EARTH'S MYSTERIOUS PLACES

EARTH'S MYSTERIOUS PLACES

THE READER'S DIGEST ASSOCIATION, INC.

Pleasantville, New York/Montreal

Quest for the Unknown
Created, edited, and designed by DK Direct Limited

A Dorling Kindersley Book

DK Direct Limited

Series Editor Richard Williams
Senior Editor Ellen Dupont; **Editor** Maxine Lewis
Editorial Research Julie Whitaker

Senior Art Editor Susie Breen
Art Editor Mark Batley; **Designer** Sara Hill
Senior Picture Researcher Frances Vargo; **Picture Assistant** Sharon Southren

Editorial Director Jonathan Reed; **Design Director** Ed Day
Production Manager Ian Paton

Volume Consultant Paul Devereux
Commissioning Editor Peter Brookesmith
Contributors John Billingsley, Dr. H. A. W. Burl, James G. Cowan,
Paul Devereux, Tom Graves, Robert Kiener, Dr. E. C. Krupp, Prof. G. T. Meaden,
Nigel Pennick, Dr. Anne Ross, Jeff Saward, Mark Valentine

Illustrators Roy Flooks, Tracey Hughes, Gary Marsh,
Coral Mula, Steve Rawlings, Indra Sharma
Photographers Simon Farnhell, Andrew Garner,
Mark Hamilton, Paul Venning, Alex Wilson

Library of Congress Cataloging in Publication Data

Earth's mysterious places.
     p.   cm. — (Quest for the unknown)
   "A Dorling Kindersley book" — T.p. verso.
   Includes index.
   ISBN 0-89577-470-4
   1. Supernatural. 2. Parapsychology. 3. Sacred space—
Miscellanea. 4. Curiosities and wonders. 5. Antiquities—
Miscellanea. I. Reader's Digest Association. II. Series.
BF1031.E29 1992
001.9'4—dc20   92-34961

Printed in the United States of America

FOREWORD

ROM THE EARLIEST TIMES, OUR ANCESTORS were drawn to certain places on the earth where they felt a presence, a momentary contact with something that they sensed as divine. These sites were sometimes characterized by such phenomena as peculiar noises, strange lights, earthquakes, or volcanic activity. This volume analyzes the attraction of many of these places, including the Serpent Mound and Chaco Canyon in the United States, England's Stonehenge, Delphi in Greece, Ayers Rock in Australia, Externsteine in Germany, and Carnac in France.

Such mysterious places wield a seemingly inexplicable power over the human psyche. For centuries they have fascinated antiquarians and mystics, but now scientists are using the latest technology to try to find the answers to the mysteries they present. For example, researchers have found that enhanced levels of radiation and electromagnetism are measurable at some sacred sites — but they are still struggling to explain why this is so. Other researchers have used low-flying planes and orbiting satellites to discover strange lines and large-scale drawings on the landscape — yet they cannot explain why the earthbound ancients drew images that can be appreciated only from the air. Archeologists have used computers and radiocarbon dating to try to unlock the secrets of ancient cities and temples — but much of the knowledge of the people who constructed these buildings remains hidden in their silent stones.

This volume examines the work that astronomers, archeologists, anthropologists, and other scientists have carried out at some of the earth's most mysterious places. It also provides examples of the strange experiences that have led many people to believe that the ancients were not only aware of the powers present at these sites but also knew how to make use of them in their daily life, rituals, and ceremonies. In our quest for the unknown we should strive to understand these mysterious sites. They are among the few remaining keys to the secrets of our ancestors.

— The Editors

CONTENTS

THE HEART OF THE WORLD

High in the mountains of Colombia in South America live a people untouched by modern civilization. Their priests believe that they are the guardians of the health of the world. Their message to the outside world: Our earth is being destroyed by greed.

Alan Ereira is an English filmmaker who embarked on a two-year quest to make a film about an enigmatic people, the Kogi, who live in an inaccessible mountainous region near the coast of Colombia in South America. These people have been trying to remain hidden for almost 500 years. But now, believing that the planet is being destroyed by the activities of modern, industrialized society, they have decided to come out of hiding and deliver their important message to the rest of the world.

The ancestors of the Kogi, the Taironas, lived in harmony with nature. They built stone cities that have been swallowed up by the dense jungle. But their buildings were so carefully planned, with an eye to drainage and resistance to erosion, that 400 years later they still stand and could be reoccupied at any time.

The way of life of the Taironas was shattered by the Spanish, who pillaged the New World for gold and enslaved its people. Many were killed or died later of diseases contracted from the Spanish. Others fled into the impenetrable heights of the mountain that rises from the sea near the city of Santa Marta, named the Sierra Nevada de Santa Marta. Four centuries later, their descendants, the Kogi, still live there, in perfect harmony with the world around them.

The story of the Kogi

What follows is Alan Ereira's account of the Kogi. He believes that modern society has much to learn from these people and therefore brought their story to the world in a television documentary called *The Heart of the World*, which he made for the BBC. He also wrote a book of the same name. This is his story:

❝The Spanish never really subdued the mountain. Even today parts of it are almost impenetrable. Much of the terrain is too steep for mules. If you do not have the help of the Indians, the distance you can travel is limited and the going is slow.

"As an ecological laboratory, rich in all life forms, the Sierra Nevada de Santa Marta is intriguing enough. But it has a greater significance. Columbus and his successors, the European invaders of America, destroyed the world they found.

The civilisations of America crumbled and vanished as Europe advanced. Only here are there towns, cities, farms, priests, temples, dances and education carrying on along lines established before Columbus came: towns without the wheel, farmers without the plough, educators without the written word, priests with the power of government. The Sierra is not just a reserve for wildlife: it is a philosophical reserve,

> The ancestors of the Kogi, the Taironas, lived in harmony with nature. Their way of life was shattered by the Spanish, who pillaged the New World for gold.

home of a society which guards the mental landscape which Europeans reworked all over the rest of the Americas. This is the land of the Kogi, the people who call themselves the Elder Brothers of humanity.

The Younger Brothers

"We are their Younger Brothers. They see us as primitive and backward, and themselves as the guardians of profound knowledge. They speak of us not as *hermanos menores*, which would simply mean 'younger brothers', but as *hermanitos menores*, a diminutive, 'very little brothers'. They recognise our technological skills, and appreciate the usefulness of some of what we make, but anything which represents a threat to the way in which they live (including our clothing and transport) is firmly rejected.

"Fundamental to that survival is the maintenance of a physical separation between their world and our own. Every intrusion made into their territory — by tourists, by anthropologists, by robbers, by peasants, by seekers after wisdom or

profit — is a threat. They are hidden, and have developed a culture of silence and secrecy. Communication with the outside world is taboo: children are taught to hide from strangers and adults regard all outsiders as dangerous. Everything about the Kogi is concealed.

Guardians of the earth

"It is a fundamental belief among the Kogi that they are the guardians of life on earth. That is what it means to be an Elder Brother. They order reality, and engineer the fertility and fecundity of nature. The Kogi have been sustained in this conviction by the extraordinary vitality of the Sierra Nevada, and by the powerful contrast between their own well managed landscape and the havoc at the foot of the mountain.

"The Mamas run this world as priests and judges. They are the educated people, masters (and mistresses, for there

are female Mamas) of the Law of the Mother. They are specialists; although they have the same core knowledge, they have from childhood developed their own areas of expertise and concern. Thus one Mama may have particular knowledge of a group of birds and animals, another of history, another may be particularly concerned with harmony in the community and so on.

Aluna: the spirit world

"The Mamas neither submit humbly to gods nor cast spells to control them; they work in *aluna*, interacting with the ocean of spirit that is all life.

"Everything is an event not only in the physical world but also in the spirit world. Every tree, every stone, every river, has a spirit form, invisible to the Younger Brother. This is the world of *aluna*, the world of thought and spirit. *Aluna* embraces intelligence, soul and fertility: it is the stuff of life, the essence of reality. The material world is underpinned, shaped, given life and generative power in *aluna*, and the Mama's work is carried out in *aluna*.

"We have no grasp of this. We see only the dream world, the shadow world of materials. That is why we are unable to grasp the significance of our actions, or understand their effects.

"The shape and nature of the physical world, its processes of birth, growth and decay, are dependent on a complex ordering in *aluna*, and the function of humanity is to try to sustain the perfect harmony of that ordering.

Walkways in *aluna*

"The physical layout of the town also constitutes a spiritual geography. The ancient path through the town, which joins the two parts of the river, is also a path in *aluna*, a special route into the spirit world for those who know how to work in *aluna*.

"The Kogi walk all the time, criss-crossing the Sierra on their way from farm to farm, from town to town. This is a vital part of the life of the Sierra. Movement from one area to another, carrying produce and seeds, stones and shells, is essential to the harmony of life. The roads were made by the ancestors, hundreds of miles of them, and they are sacred, and must be maintained, and must be walked.

> # The ancient path through the town, which joins the two parts of the river, is also a path in *aluna*, a special route into the spirit world.

"The Kogi people walk, literally as well as figuratively, in the paths of their ancestors. [There is] a powerful sense of thousands of individual trajectories constantly crossing and recrossing the mountains, weaving an astonishingly dense web of relations between kin and places, and all these movements following the well-trodden paths paved by the ancestors.

"Tairona stone-work, paving and terracing is everywhere, and there are many carved stones along the paths. Traces of the ancestors are scattered liberally around – and for the Kogi that includes mountains and large rocks as well as archaeological sites. These features are places of communication with the spirit world.

"The Kogi see the whole of the Sierra as a single entity, a sacred world in the heart of the larger world. Indeed, they call it the Heart of the World. They have to maintain the harmony of the Heart of the World by making offerings, which they call 'payments', at a multitude of sites. If this is not done, then the harmony of the Heart of the World is upset and the larger world too becomes chaotic. Archaeology digs holes in sacred sites and removes the objects that have been placed there, and that is no different from any other type of plundering. The consequences are just as devastating whether the sacred gold ends up in a museum in Bogota or a private collection in Berlin.

The end of the world
"To the Kogi it has always been clear what will happen when the world ends. The Last Trump, the signal for final destruction, will be heard at the moment when the Younger Brother reoccupies the heart of the world....That moment, when Columbus reaches his final goal,

will be the death of the Mamas and the descent of the world into chaos. The balance of nature will be overthrown.

"It is only now that the Heart of the World is being seriously threatened – not by penetration but by the effects of what is taking place lower down. Our society presses them ever harder, and has cut them off from the sea. At the same moment, we heat up the world. They say we are doing this by cutting down the trees and by digging the minerals in the earth. That is why they have to warn us.

"The world is growing hotter. And the heat is a sign of serious problems. Its causes are manifold, but all the causes can be traced to the Younger Brother and the way he treats the earth. One of the clearest causes is the cutting down of trees. By stripping the land of trees, the Younger Brother takes away the water in the land and dries it. Then the sun will heat it and parch it.

Changing our ways
"The Kogi make no predictions. They say only that if we do not change, they believe the world will die. It will cease to be fertile. They say that their work is futile in the face of our destruction.

"They do not ask us to be like them, but they do say that we must stop taking fuels from the ground in the way we do, and we must stop tearing trees from the earth in the way we do. More than that, we need to become sensitised to the life of the earth. And we must leave them alone. They need access to the sea, they need to recover a corridor of land that will give them that, and they need to have their ancestral sites protected from tomb-robbers. Apart from that, they want only silence. They need very little from us, except to be left in peace. **"**

Extracts taken from *The Heart of the World* by Alan Ereira, published by Jonathan Cape Ltd, London, 1990. A fee has been paid to the Tairona Heritage Trust for the use of this material.

The Kogi say that
we must stop
taking fuels from
the ground and
tearing trees from
the earth. And we
must leave their
people alone.
They need to
have their
ancestral sites
protected from
tomb-robbers.
Apart from that
they need very
little from us,
except to be left
in peace.

COMMENT

We have chosen the story of the Kogi Indians as our introduction because their way of life epitomizes a relationship between the earth and humankind that was common in the ancient world, but is rare today. Unlike the inhabitants of the industrialized world, the Kogi have maintained a unique and unchanged relationship with their landscape, which they believe is sacred and powerful.

Their lives center on a basic belief in the spiritual world, *aluna*, which they see as a direct continuation of the physical world. The Kogi holy men and women, the Mamas, believe that every action takes place in the spiritual world as well as in the physical one. Their maps, which were carved on stones by their ancestors, the Taironas, show lines that represent both the stone paths and stairways of their jungle fastness and the flights of mind of which the Kogi Mamas are thought to be capable in their travels in *aluna*.

> At the end of filming, the Kogi once again closed the bridge that provided access to their secret civilization.

Understanding sacred sites

Hidden away from the rest of the world since the 16th century, the Kogi, who have managed to preserve the traditions of their civilization, are a living example of an ancient people.

Throughout this volume we shall see many examples of sacred sites around the world, some built thousands of years ago. These earth shrines raise a number of questions. What do they mean? And how were they used by the people who built them? Perhaps studying the Kogi, and other peoples, will help us to unlock the secrets of these lost cultures.

Modern society has tended to ignore the natural and mysterious properties that the earth appears to have. Some researchers believe that prehistoric peoples, perhaps because they had to observe the world closely in order to survive, were more sensitive to the existence of powers in the earth. In this case, they may have made constructive use of their discoveries — tapping the power of place to augment the rituals that took place at their sacred sites.

Learning from the ancients

But to the Kogi, we, and not the various peoples of prehistory, are the primitive ones. They see our devotion to material objects, our reliance on science and technology, and our dependence on gadgetry (which they contemptuously call "moths") as false and damaging. Perhaps it is time, in view of the global ecological crisis, for us to review the way that we think.

Ancient peoples, like the Kogi today, utilized only the natural properties of the earth; they did not desecrate their land, they revered it. The secret mountain retreat inhabited by the Kogi has an integrity that transcends both time and culture, and therefore should be preserved for generations to come.

By permitting Alan Ereira to make his film, the Kogi have allowed us to enter their world and hear their message. We do not have to ruin the land to benefit from it. Ancient peoples, it seems, also understood this. Perhaps by learning to recognize the significance of the earth's mysterious places we may rediscover our relationship with the land around us.

Now that they have delivered their message to the world, the Kogi wish to be left in peace once more. At the end of filming, in a symbolic gesture, they once again closed the bridge that provided access to their secret civilization.

CHAPTER ONE

ENERGIES IN THE EARTH

Sacred sites are sometimes found in geophysically significant locations where strange lights and other phenomena are often reported. These phenomena, which even the latest scientific research cannot fully explain, may have attracted the ancients to these mysterious places.

Many ancient monuments are located where electrical storms are common and where strange unexplained lights reportedly appear. Others, it seems, lie above fractures or faults in the earth's crust. This has led some investigators to speculate that these ancient sites were selected because of their proximity to elemental forces of nature.

In what is now Ohio, Indians of the Hopewell and Adena cultures appear to have selected key geological areas for the

Indian Graves

Ohio Serpent Mound
The largest such effigy in the world, the Serpent Mound was built by the Adena people in about 500 B.C.

Hopewell mother
The Ohio Hopewell people (100 B.C.–A.D. 350) buried their most treasured possessions in the huge earthworks they constructed. This painted ceramic figurine of a Hopewell woman and her infant was found in a burial mound in Calhoun County, Illinois.

creation of their enormous earthworks and burial mounds. For example, in Adams County, Ohio, the heartland of the ancient Adena culture, there is a huge Serpent Mound that depicts a 1,348-foot-long uncoiling serpent whose open jaws enclose an oval earthwork. The Adena people situated this great, mysterious monument over an area of intensive geological faulting, caused either by volcanic action or meteoric impact. This area of intensive faulting seems to be unique in the whole of the United States.

The dramatic power of the elements may also have been harnessed by the builders of Teotihuacan, Mexico's 2,000-year-old Toltec city. The largest structure in the sacred city is the Pyramid of the Sun. And in 1906, archeologists found a thick layer of the mineral mica on top of it; this was subsequently lost during reconstruction. Mica has insulating properties as far as electricity is concerned, while pyramid structures in open land are known to attract atmospheric electricity. Thus some researchers have suggested that the huge statues that once topped the pyramids of Teotihuacan may have been instruments in some rudimentary form of technology involving the elements of nature.

Collision point

In A.D. 930 the people of Iceland erected their main parliament building and ceremonial center, the Althing, on a great fault — a rift valley they called Thingvellir. A dramatic feature of this place is the Almannagja, or the Rift Rock of the People. "Walking along it," describes Katherine Scherman in her 1976 book, *Iceland — Daughter of Fire*, "the sense of the earth splitting apart beneath one's feet is very strong." The rift valley is now 35 feet wider than it was when the Althing was founded, because it

sits on the mid-Atlantic Ridge, where the North American and Eurasian tectonic plates pull apart. Such plates are slabs of the earth's crust that are even larger than the continents; they float on underlying seas of molten rock. Wherever these plates collide, exceptional earthquake and volcanic activity occurs.

The Cascade Mountains in Washington State mark the spot where the Pacific and North American plates grind together, causing earthly disturbances such as the volcanic eruption of Mount Saint Helens in 1980. Farther south, the plate margin is marked by the San Andreas Fault.

In California the southernmost peak of the Cascades range of mountains, Mount Shasta, served as a holy mountain for the Wintu and other American Indian tribes of the region. In a sense these mountains still retain their mystery: The first modern "flying saucers" were witnessed in 1947

Hopewell copper burial effigy

by Kenneth Arnold as he flew over the Cascades range. He perceived bright disks flashing between Mount Rainier and Mount Adams, like saucers skimming over the surface of water. Arnold himself never believed they were extraterrestrial spacecraft. The disks may have been "earth lights," unexplained points or balls of light, which have often been reported at a variety of sites around the world, particularly those regarded as sacred.

Fault zones

Above some fault zones, various minerals and rocks have been violently mixed together, causing magnetic and electrical anomalies, and even measurable variations in gravity. Far from being fixed, gravity, magnetism, and the direction of true north on a compass may all vary at points on the surface of the earth. For example, the type of metallic ore in rock determines its magnetic properties while the thickness of the earth's crust or the altitude at a certain site can influence the gravitational force measurable there. Under tectonic pressure, fault zones can show changing energy fields too. Some researchers suggest that fault zones might possibly cause altered states of consciousness in susceptible people.

Around the world, sacred sites are time and again found to be positioned on fault lines. Just north of Flagstaff, Arizona, lies an ancient Anasazi site, Wupatki Pueblo, built over blowholes that inhale and exhale air over six-hour periods. These blowholes are openings in the earth that are connected to vast underground geological fault systems. The Anasazi and other American Indians of the southwest dug holes in the floors of their *kivas* (circular subterranean

> ## Fault zones might cause altered states of consciousness in susceptible people.

ceremonial chambers), possibly with the intention of forming entrances to the sacred underworld. At Wupatki Pueblo these holes connect directly to the blowholes beneath, which may indicate that fault systems played an essential part in Anasazi ceremonies.

Light phenomena
Some researchers believe that ancient peoples positioned sacred sites on fault lines to make use of the dramatic light effects that seem to occur at such areas. At Carnac in Brittany, for example, the thousands of standing stones, arranged in rows, are hemmed in by faults. The presence of strange lights are often reported here. In Britain large balls of white light were seen over the Castlerigg circle in 1919. Recent research by geochemist Paul

McCartney has found that many of the stone circles dotted around Britain are located within a mile or so of a fault or associated geological intrusion.

One of the areas that has had the most thorough earth light study is the Barmouth-Harlech region near Dyffryn, Wales. Here, the crucial geological factor is the Mochras fault, a deep-rooted feature that virtually links Barmouth and Harlech. In 1905 there were many reports of columns of light issuing from the ground in this area, and recent research has shown that not only did most of these events occur close to the fault, but also that the incidence increased with proximity to the fault. In fact, on a map, pointers marking the site of many of the events show them strung along the fault like beads on a thread.

In March 1991 an outbreak of light balls was reported around Nevern, a hamlet near the foot of magnetic Carn Ingli in Dyfed, Wales. The folklorist W. Y. Evans Wentz recorded in *The Fairy Faith in Celtic Countries* (1911) that the local

Thingvellir
The site of the first Icelandic parliament lies at the center of the mid-Atlantic Ridge.

Machupicchu
This granite citadel of the Incas sits on a fault line. Mysterious lights have been witnessed here on several occasions.

THE EARTHQUAKE CONNECTION

In 1986 geologist Dr. John S. Derr and neuroscientist Professor Michael Persinger of Laurentian University, Ontario, Canada, published a study of an outbreak of strange light activity at the Yakima Indian reservation in the Cascade Mountains of Washington State. They found that the most intense periods of light activity coincided with peak periods of earthquake activity in the region.

Persinger believes that "strain fields" in the earth's crust, caused by even low-intensity tectonic pressures, may pass through

Spiral stones
Many of the stones at the Newgrange burial mound in Northern Ireland are carved with spirals, the most widespread of prehistoric symbols.

Nevern folk at the turn of the century spoke of green-colored lightballs "as big as a pot." In the lore of the day, these were known as "corpse candles" and were thought to foretell an imminent death in the village. Such "earth lights," or "spook lights," are commonly reported appearing around ancient sacred sites and the geologically faulted terrain that such sites frequently occupy.

Powerful places

The power of the earth's sacred places has been known to inspire a variety of strange occurrences at the sites. Often inexplicable, these incidents reportedly include electric shocks, visions, out-of-body experiences, dizziness, and other odd sensations.

Peter Thornborrow, a British local official, had a strange experience that illustrates this phenomenon. He was walking alone through the stone circle called Long Meg and Her Daughters in Cumbria in the north of England. He suddenly felt as if he were "not really there...not really in the same time."

Mount Shasta

certain geologically sensitive areas, triggering the lights. Persinger and his colleagues have also found that an increase in the strength of the earth's magnetic field may precede outbreaks of lights. But they do not yet fully understand how this happens.

Feeling dizzy, he leaned against one of the stones, and received what felt like a powerful electric shock from it.

To anecdotes like this must be added the testimony of folklore. For generations farmers and others living in the English countryside have claimed that prehistoric standing stones possess mysterious

> Thornborrow felt as if he were "not really there, not really in the same time." Feeling dizzy, he leaned against one of the stones and received what felt like an electric shock from it.

powers — there are many stories about groups of stones that can move, heal, emit a variety of strange sounds and lights, harbor fairies and other elemental beings, and even attract lightning.

Investigating the earth's energies

This combination of modern experience and traditional lore has led many people to believe that there are unusual energies at some ancient sites. Most mainstream archeologists have been reluctant to accept or even investigate this idea, but other people have attempted to study it. Since the turn of the century, psychics have surveyed these sites, and since the 1930's, dowsers (who claim to be able to

Castlerigg, England
Set against a skyline of rugged hills, Castlerigg has been the setting for many strange light phenomena.

BALL LIGHTNING

For centuries, scientists have debated the existence of "ball lightning" — brightly colored globes of light seen floating in the sky during or after thunderstorms. Recent research conducted by two Japanese scientists suggests that ball lightning may indeed be a real meteorological phenomenon.

LIGHTNING MAY BE THOUGHT OF as a huge, sudden spark of electricity generated by the difference in electricity between particles of matter — for example, between opposite charges within two clouds. The discharge follows the line of least resistance, which often forms a forked pattern. In addition to normal fork lightning, however, thousands of people in the United States and Europe claim to have seen luminous spheres moving through the air during or after thunderstorms — so-called ball lightning.

Fact or folklore?
Ball lightning may be white, orange, blue, or red, and is said to vary enormously in size, from grape to basketball. Such lightning is often accompanied by a loud hissing sound. Some eyewitnesses claim that ball lightning is capable of passing through walls and moving against the wind. According to some accounts, it can cause damage by burning or melting various materials; others maintain that it is quite harmless. It reportedly dies out suddenly, either silently or explosively, a few seconds after it first appears.

Unlike normal lightning, ball lightning appears to occur without any apparent contact between oppositely charged particles, thus defying ordinary physical principles. Its occurrence is therefore much more difficult to explain. Many scientists used to dismiss ball lightning as an illusion. For example, in 1839 the British physicist Michael Faraday (1791–1867), whose experiments form much of the foundation for our understanding of the forces of electricity and magnetism,

theorized that ball lightning might simply be an after-image formed by the human eye following initial exposure to the flash of ordinary fork lightning.

But the Soviet scientist Pyotr Kapitsa, winner of the Nobel Prize for physics in 1978, disagreed. He suggested that ball lightning was indeed a true, physical phenomenon. He proposed that the luminous globes consisted of plasma — matter composed of electrically charged atomic particles stimulated by natural radio waves to generate light. Recent experiments by two Japanese physicists appear to support this view. Some experts, however, are still not convinced and maintain that the precise nature of ball lightning remains unexplained.

The Japanese experiments
In 1989, Yoshi-hiko Ohtsuki of Waseda University and H. Ofuruton of Tokyo Metropolitan College of Aeronautical Engineering reported that they had created ball lightning in the laboratory. Using a magnetron (a generator of microwave radiation) connected by a special guide wire to a copper cavity, they were able to create small regions of concentrated energy within the cavity. The experiments yielded different types of balls of varying colors. One type of ball occurred only rarely throughout the experiments; the scientists suggested that this might be a plasma vortex.

Scientific support
Following the revelations of the Japanese scientists, Dr. Stanley Singer, chairman of the International Committee for Ball Lightning Research, announced that their experiments "were a considerable advance over any previous studies." However, if ball lightning does consist of plasma, as many scientists now believe, further work is needed to identify the forces that hold it in a sphere.

A natural lightning ball
This snapshot, taken by amateur photographer Werner Burger in St. Gallenkirch, Montafon Valley, Austria, in 1978, is probably the only color photograph of a natural lightning ball in existence. Its authenticity has been verified by several experts, including Dr. Alexander Keul of the University of Salzburg in Austria.

locate substances or energies, most often beneath the surface of the earth or water, using a hand-held instrument such as a rod or pendulum) have tried to establish patterns of energy at them. But because both of these approaches can be highly subjective, findings at the various sites have been largely inconclusive.

Blanche Mertz, a Swiss earth energies researcher, has tried to introduce greater objectivity to the study of natural energies at given locations. She studies

---

Witnesses have reported seeing: a car containing two people disappear as it approached the stone circle; a huge, doglike creature with gray hair appear fleetingly and then vanish....

---

ancient sites using a variety of scientific instruments, including a geiger counter, which measures levels of radiation, and a biometer, a specialized device designed to evaluate the dowsing reaction. A biometer is a type of dowsing pendulum with a calibrated scale that measures the dowsing response in terms of wavelengths (angstrom units) or frequencies (gigahertz). Although the biometer attempts to test the dowser's skill objectively, it is still a very subjective method. For although dowsing does sometimes appear to work, how it works remains a mystery even to dowsers.

The Dragon Project, a British earth energies research group, has also tested dowsers and psychics. Yet their results, too, have been inconclusive. The group also monitors physical effects at various megalithic monument sites throughout the British Isles, searching for possible physical energy explanations for some of the anecdotes and legends associated with these sites. They have studied such forces as magnetism, radioactivity, radiation, sound waves, and even the electrical characteristics of the stones.

Measuring radioactivity

At Long Meg in Cumbria they discovered that a few of the standing stones at the site contained small areas or nodes that emitted continuous streams of gamma radiation. These were the same stones that reportedly gave Peter Thornborrow his shock. While granite is usually slightly radioactive, these standing stones are unusual in that they appear to possess concentrated points of energy.

Radiation itself may not have been the cause of Peter Thornborrow's reported disorientation. Dragon Project researchers, however, have discovered that zones of heightened natural radiation at ancient sites, caused by the presence of granite or other radioactive minerals, or an issue of radon gas from the ground, may have an effect on sensitive individuals.

At the Rollright stone circle near Oxford, England, a series of measurements revealed that a 1,000-foot length of the lane adjacent to it produces higher-than-normal background geiger counts. One possible explanation is that this might be caused by energy-emitting rocks in the road's foundation.

That specific stretch of road near the Rollright stones has been the site of many curious

__Long Meg and Her Daughters__
According to local legend, the stones in this prehistoric circle in Cumbria, England, are the petrified remains of witches who dared to dance on the Sabbath.

experiences. Among these, witnesses have reported seeing: a car containing two people disappear as it approached the stone circle; a huge, doglike creature with coarse gray hair appear fleetingly and then vanish; and an old-fashioned gypsy caravan that appeared and then just as suddenly disappeared. Although these strange sightings at the site might be explained away as mere optical illusions or simple misunderstandings, the people involved seemed to believe that the sightings were part of some sort of hallucinatory effect caused by the site's mysterious properties.

The effect of radiation

Other unexplained effects occur at sites that appear to exhibit enhanced natural radiation. Most of Europe's underground chambers are found in areas with a high proportion of granite rocks or where stones with some degree of uranium in them have been found. Inside a 5,000-year-old Cornish dolmen (a type of monument that consists of two or more upright stones supporting a horizontal slab), British archeologist John Barnatt and a photographer, Brian Larkman, saw bands of light flashing along the bottom of the horizontal slab. Geiger counter readings that were significantly higher than normal background readings have reportedly been recorded at the dolmen.

Some researchers, including Blanche Mertz, believe that ancient builders were aware of the effects of radiation and chose sites in order to make use of "the play of natural forces."

Using radiation

The King's Chamber in Egypt's Great Pyramid is faced with granite. Studies there have revealed enhanced radiation levels, apparently caused by the buildup of radiation in the enclosure. Radiation itself was not discovered until 1896, but the builders of the Egyptian pyramids may have known of its effects and it is possible that they deliberately created the heightened radiation levels that have been found in the King's Chamber.

Holy wells can be mildly radioactive, as well. The thermal mineral springs at Bath, England, which have been used as healing waters for some 7,000 years, are mildly radioactive, as are the waters of the Chalice Well, Glastonbury. Above-average geiger counter readings have also been recorded at a number of Celtic holy wells in Great Britain and Ireland.

Magnetic attraction

Stones and sacred sites have been tested for magnetic anomalies (local variations in the earth's magnetic field). At Carn Ingli in Wales, places where compass needles point south instead of north have been found, indicating areas of strong magnetic deviation. At Castlerigg, a stone circle in the north of England, only the westernmost stone, of 38 stones at the circle, affects a compass needle. A natural outcrop of serpentine rock at an American Indian place of power on Mount Tamalpais outside San Francisco also reportedly causes the needles of compasses placed at the site to spin uncontrollably.

In the Namoratunga II complex of stone circles and rows found near Lake Turkana, Kenya, several researchers from Michigan State University discovered that some stones were highly magnetic and strongly affected compasses and magnetic equipment used in the immediate area. Since the rows of stones point to the four cardinal compass points, several researchers have speculated that the ancient builders of the site may have been aware of the magnetism present there.

In addition to these magnetic effects, due solely to geological factors in the rocks, members of the Dragon Project, using sensitive magnetometers, have found that some of the stones at a variety of British sites apparently produce inexplicable, sudden fluctuations of low-level magnetic emissions. These fluctuations can last for several hours. Similar

Testing magnetism
A scientist in Australia uses a sun compass and a magnetometer to detect magnetic anomalies at the Great Wall, Lake Mungo.

Ancient earthquake theories
This Aztec statue depicts the sun god Tonatiuh, with a symbol of the earthquake on his back. According to the Aztecs, the world will end with an earthquake.

magnetic effects at the Rollright stone circle, in Oxfordshire, England, were reported in the magazine *New Scientist* in 1983. Geologists cannot explain why these magnetic pulses occur.

Strange sounds

Unexplained sounds, too, seem to occur at some ancient sites. Ringing noises have been heard at Stonehenge, while at the Rollright stone circle witnesses have reported curious clicking noises emanating from the area of ground around the stones in the middle of the night.

Ultrasound — high-frequency sound beyond normal human hearing, such as that produced by dog whistles — might cause this phenomenon. When the stones at some of the sites are tested with an ultrasound receiver, seemingly odd effects are reported. Researchers testing the Rollright stone circle found that a three-foot band around the middle of the tallest stone of the circle allegedly gave off a signal at dawn that affected an ultrasound receiver. The signal ebbed away later in the day. Explanations offered for such sounds are that they might be produced by secret military telecommunications signals that resonate in the stones, or they might be the creation of some still unknown geophysical effect.

Area of curious sounds

But these effects are not unique to Great Britain. Mount Tom, on the east bank of the Connecticut River in East Haddam, Connecticut, was sacred to the Pequot and other Indian tribes of the region. Their name for the site was *Machemoodus*, which means, "there is a bad noise." It is one of the most seismically active places in New England — in colonial times it was known as an area of curious sounds, called the Moodus noises. Sounds like guns, drums, and

The Blind Fiddler
Muffled thunderclaps have reportedly been heard emanating from beneath the earth at the 11-foot-tall Blind Fiddler stone in Cornwall, England.

The San Andreas Fault
The fault exhibits many magnetic anomalies.

rumbling have been heard at the site at times when earthquakes and other forms of seismic upheaval occurred.

Crystal power

Crystals have long been thought to have certain mystical powers, such as healing, interacting with the mind, and even preventing drunkenness. They often play an important role in ritual and religion. Twentieth century science and medicine, however, give them little credence.

During initiation ceremonies among the Australian Aborigines, small crystals, known as solidified lights, were inserted beneath the skin of young men. For the Indian tribes of New England, quartz boulders or rocks with quartz seams were *manitou-aseniah*, or "spirit stones."

Underlying the religious significance of crystals are their electromagnetic properties. At Duloe, Cornwall, the stones in the circle are huge blocks of white quartz, one of which has reportedly been known to give off electric shocks. There may also be a crystal connection at other prehistoric sites, suggesting that ancient

▶ PAGE 28

DAWN SONG

Uncanny sounds are an odd feature of a few of the world's ancient, sacred sites. In Egypt, eerie sounds once emanated from the gigantic Colossi of Memnon.

The northernmost of the two statues began to make curious sounds at dawn. People flocked to the site, believing the sounds to be the voice of an oracle.

UNEXPLAINED NOISES and even recognizable musical notes can sometimes be made by striking certain rocks. These natural stone-age percussion instruments ring when struck with a mallet or even with the knuckles.

In the Upper Black Eddy area of Pennsylvania, there is an entire field of rocks, about a third of which actually ring. Scientists theorize that over many centuries, the interaction of the weather and the geography of the field itself may have altered the structure of certain rocks, allowing these rocks to resonate at easily audible frequencies when they are struck.

But some stones do not have to be struck in order to make sounds. The gigantic Colossi of Memnon are two statues that form the last remnants of a temple that stood between Luxor and the Valley of the Kings in ancient Egypt. The northernmost of the two huge statues began to make curious sounds when it was cracked during an earthquake in 27 B.C. It began producing an audible, bell-like sound at dawn. People flocked to the site from far and wide, believing the sounds to be the voice of an oracle. The strange sounds stopped when the cracks were repaired in A.D. 350.

Ancient ultrasound

Modern commentators suggest that such sounds may have been caused by wind blowing through the cracks. Another theory is that the statues emitted high-frequency ultrasound signals that were made audible to humans only by the structural damage resulting from the earthquake. Some Egyptologists have come up with the highly speculative theory that the ancient builders might have incorporated sonic factors into their structures because they were aware of the healing properties of ultrasound. The use of ultrasound to heal bruised tissue is now a widely accepted medical technique.

Colossal statue
One of the two 60-foot-tall statues of the Egyptian king Amenhotep III that are all that remains of his mortuary temple. These are known as the Colossi of Memnon. Each figure of the king is flanked by the smaller figures of his mother and his wife.

SUBTERRANEAN STATES

The ionization process represents a change of electrical charge in the atmosphere. Some speculate that positive and negative ions may have various effects on states of consciousness. Negative ions occur near waterfalls, breaking waves, in areas that contain uranium deposits, and in caves. Such powerfully ionized zones often surround the kinds of places recognized as holy by ancient and traditional peoples.

The Aranda shamanic initiates of central Australia, for example, slept in the mouths of caves, hoping that the spirits would come and transport them into the interior of the caves, where they believed paradise lay.

Lightning strikes

There is a high incidence of lightning strikes due to ionization at cave mouths. Earlier in this century, an explorer at the Henne-Morte caverns in France was struck by lightning 200 feet below ground. Intense ionization in caves may be caused by radioactivity from subterranean rock formations accumulating by the action of groundwater. The radiation builds up in the enclosed cavern and is sometimes expelled during hot, summery weather, sending a stream of ionization skyward and thus providing a path for lightning.

peoples used crystals in their ceremonial activities. Inside the 5,000-year-old chamber at Gavrinis, Brittany, there is a block of quartz that apparently glows brightly only at key points in the lunar calendar. Some researchers believe that the builders of the chamber were aware of this effect and strategically positioned the quartz crystal there.

Although the geology of some ancient sacred sites can be charted, the effect that such sites may have had on the mind is more difficult to quantify. In 1980 British psychic Ken Shaw took part in a test to investigate the interactions between various minerals and the operations of the mind. For example, Shaw positioned his hands six inches above a piece of quartz that was attached to a molecular resonance meter (a machine that can detect changes in the way the molecules in the stone bond together) and visualized healing energy streaming into it. The digital readout on the resonance meter reportedly began to tumble chaotically. When Shaw stopped visualizing the streaming energy, the reading settled down. He was able to reproduce the effect each time he tried the test.

Energy effects

Using special scientific equipment, some earth mysteries researchers have been able to measure objectively a variety of anomalies at ancient sacred sites. Extensive research at the ancient stone site of

One of Carnac's intricately carved stones

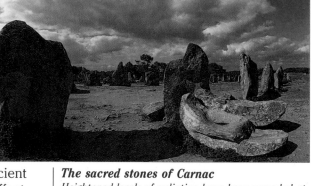

The sacred stones of Carnac
Heightened levels of radiation have been recorded at the ancient stones at Carnac in Brittany, France.

Carnac in France by researcher Pierre Méreaux, and at the Rollright stone circle in England by the Dragon Project, has provided evidence of strange energy effects at these sacred sites. Additional scientific research at other sites might help prove or disprove the existence of such strange phenomena.

Crystal powerhouse of Callanish
At one stone circle in Callanish, Scotland, crystals such as quartz, feldspar, or hornblende are found in almost every stone.

The Power of Ancient Stones

"As he trailed his fingers across the lintel stone above his head at the opening of the long, low passage into the mound, he received a powerful electric shock."

ACK ROBERTS, A STUDENT of ancient astronomy, was conducting experiments at Newgrange, a chambered burial mound in Northern Ireland, to try to unravel the mysteries of a unique spectacle that occurs there at dawn on the winter solstice every year. At that moment a finger of light shines down the long passageway and hits the back wall of the end chamber. As the light falls on the back wall, it illuminates richly decorated stones across whose faces double spirals wind, clockwise to one side and counterclockwise to the other. This amazing prehistoric light show can still be witnessed at the site today, although the sun has changed its slant by an entire degree since the burial mound was first built around 3000 B.C.

A shocking experience

Arriving at the site one May morning, Roberts paused before entering the ancient chambered burial mound. As he trailed his fingers across the lintel stone above his head at the opening of the long, low passage into the mound, he received a powerful electric shock that numbed his arm. It felt, he remembered later, like a strong discharge of static electricity. Roberts recoiled momentarily before gingerly reaching up to touch the stone again. This time, however, nothing happened. Whatever force had given him the shock was spent.

Roberts was not the first person to receive a shock at Newgrange. On another occasion dowser John Williams received a similar shock when he touched both ends of a double spiral simultaneously.

These interlinking spirals are carved across the faces of many of the stones at Newgrange. They may represent maps of other burial sites in the area, or be symbols of underground water lines,

the Celtic triple goddess Brigid, or even the life force itself. Supporters of the life force theory point to the discoveries of modern biology and physics: the double-helix structure of DNA and the spiraling galaxies of the universe whose whirling power gives birth to stars. The molecular structure of quartz is also a spiral and the entire mound is faced with quartz stones. One peculiar feature of quartz crystal is its apparent ability to give off a significant electrical charge under certain conditions.

The spiral symbol is the one found most commonly at prehistoric sites around the world. Thus it is possible to speculate that ancient peoples may have had some awareness of its significance.

DOWSING THE EARTH'S FORCES

In recent decades, dowsers have been working at many prehistoric sites around the world. In the process, they have directed archeologists to a number of significant finds — and opened a whole new chapter of earth mysteries.

NEW WORLD MYSTERIES

Back home after a research trip in Britain, two dowsers went for a drive in Mount Tamalpais State Park, just north of San Francisco. They stopped at a lookout point above the Pacific Ocean. Known as the Flight Stones, the point is a stone outcrop once sacred to the Miwok Indians but now used as a

The Flight Stones

launch point for hang gliders. Although the stones are almost certainly a natural formation, the dowsers were reminded of a stone circle they had dowsed in England. Intrigued, they used their dowsing rods and found that they showed the same patterns of movement on the California cliff.

They reportedly sensed lines of water weaving between the stones as well as straight paths above the ground. Whatever strange forces were involved, the dowsers felt able to conclude that their theories were not limited to the standing stones of the Old World.

MANY DOWSERS CLAIM to be able to sense and map strange energy lines and grids that surround and even link prehistoric sites. Yet verifying their claims in scientific terms is virtually impossible for two reasons. Conventional science does not accept the validity of dowsing nor does it believe in the existence of bizarre energies in the earth.

Since Roman times, dowsing has provided clues to the existence and location of water hidden beneath the earth's surface. Roman dowsers used a twisted loop of willow, known as a *lituus*, as a dowsing rod. Throughout the centuries, dowsing has also been used to search for various metal ores and oil hidden beneath the ground.

It is easy enough to test the accuracy of a metal or water dowser simply by digging at the precise spot the dowser indicates. Prediction of the existence of water or minerals under the earth has none of the vagueness of a prediction concerning the supposed presence of energy lines. In fact, many professional water-finders are so confident of their skill that they are even willing to work on a "no water, no pay" basis.

During the 1930's, dowsers began to explore ancient sacred sites. Two French water diviners, Louis Merle and Charles Diot, used dowsing to scan several ancient burial mounds in France. They mapped clusterings of what they called "water lines," which they believed were underground streams. Dowsers in other countries found similar water lines at other ancient sacred sites.

A well-known British dowser of the 1930's, Captain F. L. M. Boothby, even suggested that "the whole layout of these ancient monuments is based on subterranean water," but he warned that until all the sites had been fully surveyed this theory could not be proven.

The ley connection

However, many dowsers claim to find more than water at prehistoric sacred sites. They claim to be able to detect and map lines of energy lying not only between individual stones at a site but even between entire sites.

WHAT IS DOWSING?

Dowsing is the ability to locate something, most often beneath the surface of the earth or water, using a hand-held instrument, such as a rod or a pendulum.

The basic principle is simple: dowsers watch and interpret their body's involuntary reactions to the environment. In dowsing, these "body responses" show up as small movements of the hands. Dowsers generally use some kind

Psychic power at work?
Dowsing from maps cannot be explained by physical forces such as magnetism acting on the body.

of tool to make those reactions more visible: a bent twig, a simple lever, a weight on a thread, or a twisted piece of grass.

The dowsing rod itself moves not because it possesses any magical properties but because the hands move. But no one knows why the hands move. Research suggests that minute changes in natural energies, such as magnetism and radiation, may affect the body and trigger the dowsing reflex.

Interpretation

Once the dowser gets a response, he or she must then be able to interpret the movements of the rod in order to visualize what lies beneath the ground. At a large prehistoric site, for example, there are reportedly many different kinds of influences and energies: underground springs, magnetism or radiation in the stones, and even what dowsers call ghosts: traces of actions and emotions that once occurred there.

The old straight track
This Welsh ley at Llanthony, Gwent, leads through the old priory and up the hill.

LEY LINES

The term "ley" was first used by Alfred Watkins in the 1920's to designate deliberate alignments of ancient sacred sites. He believed that the leys were tracks used by merchants; straight lines that led point to point across Britain.

Recent research has shown that such alignments, as well as other kinds of linear features in ancient landscapes, were deliberately created by ancient peoples. Their reasons for doing so, however, are lost in the mists of time.

Leys fascinated Britain's psychic researchers, who believed that they held the key to understanding ancient sites. Many of them came to believe that leys were more than just tracks, as they led across impassable terrain, such as bogs.

Lines of force

Leys were first called lines of force after Alfred Watkins's death, in a novel entitled *The Goat-Foot God* (1936), by occultist Dion Fortune. At the same time, French and German dowsers began to speak of "energy grids" crisscrossing the earth's surface, an ancient power grid, they believed, that prehistoric peoples may have tapped into to gain access to spiritual energies. These are the grids that modern dowsers claim to detect, although measurements and features may vary from one grid to another.

This energy theory was first developed in 1938 by dowser Arthur Lawton, who combined the idea of grid patterns and subterranean water lines with Alfred Watkins's theory about leys, and said that the energy patterns could be dowsed. In the 1950's French author Aimé Michel noted that low-level UFO's were often reported traveling along straight lines, which he called "orthotenies." In 1961 Tony Wedd, an ex-RAF pilot and UFO enthusiast, read about orthotenies and equated them with leys. He suggested that orthotenies were straight lines of magnetic energy used by UFO's for refueling.

The pattern of the past

During the 1950's, leading British dowser Guy Underwood identified three further dowsable patterns of underground water lines. He called these lines "aquastats," "geostats," and "tracklines."

In his book *The Pattern of the Past* (1969), he claimed that these coincided closely with many features of British sites such as Stonehenge, Salisbury cathedral, the "White Horse" hill figure at Uffington, and sections of some ancient roadways. According to Underwood, these patterns had always existed, and the sites had been chosen and the standing stones placed over the springs deliberately. But if this is the case, why were these springs so important?

Bill Lewis, Tom Graves, and other dowsers claimed that dowsing patterns could also be found on the surfaces of standing stones and above ground between stones, or even between sites. This suggested that leys were lines of energy, not just ancient

Pointing in the right direction
Detail of "cup" and "directional line" markings on a stone in a complex of leys on Rombald's Moor, Yorkshire, England.

roads. The dowsable lines that Graves called "overgrounds" seemed to coincide with ley alignments between sites, which are now often described as energy leys.

In recent years, discoveries of energy leys have proliferated. In various parts of the U.S.A., Germany, France, and New Zealand some dowsers claim to find grid-like patterns along with water lines. In Britain and Australia, people have found symbols like Maltese crosses, or shapes echoing those seen in the crop circles, while others claim to have found lines that interweave for hundreds of miles.

Energy grids

The idea that grids or networks of energy encircle the globe is an extension of this energy-line theory. One well-known grid was discovered by a German physician named Ernst Hartmann in the 1950's. He believed that energy rays rising from the earth in invisible walls could be dowsed to reveal a grid pattern. Each grid square is said to measure $6\frac{1}{2}$ feet by 8 feet. Hartmann believed that this grid network covered the whole globe.

But Hartmann was not the only energy dowser to discover a grid pattern. Other researchers claim to have detected new and different patterns, which they believe can be found throughout the world. They include the Peyre Grid, the Curry Net, and the Harvalik Grid, as well as a host of recent "New Age" additions. Individual dowsers tend to fit the energies that they detect to the particular grid pattern that

▸ PAGE 34

DOWSING AT THE STONES

Dowsers claim to be able to divine mysterious energy patterns at ancient sites; but when put to the test, a number of dowsers were unable to agree on what lay beneath a group of standing stones.

AFTER FRENCH WATER DIVINERS claimed to find crossing streams of underground water beneath burial mounds in the 1930's, many dowsers tried dowsing at ancient sites of all kinds.

They initially claimed to find water beneath the sites, but in the 1950's British dowser Guy Underwood claimed to find other features he called "track lines" and "aquastats," which he felt were not caused by water. Nowadays dowsers claim to be able to find all kinds of supposed "earth energies" at ancient monuments.

On a more accountable level, energy dowsers sometimes assist archeologists engaged in excavations in finding specific features. Dowsing may also be used to survey a large site before digging begins. In Britain, for example, one energy dowser claimed to be able to sense a concrete structure lying beneath London's Kensington Barracks. This sounded implausible until excavations for restorative work uncovered the original concrete foundations of a long-forgotten Roman barracks hidden beneath the 18th-century building.

Testing the dowsers

The Rollright stone circle, near Oxford, England, has been the main base of the Dragon Project, an enterprise run by enthusiasts who investigate rumors of strange energy effects at a variety of prehistoric monuments. In a series of experiments in 1980, the claims of dowsers were scientifically evaluated there as a part of a comprehensive inquiry run by the project.

Individual dowsers were given plans of the site and asked to plot underground watercourses at specific depths. The results they obtained rarely matched one another. Dowsers were also asked to detect any buried features. But they could reach no agreement when estimating the numbers of human burials at the stone circle — in fact, their estimates ranged from six to over a thousand! Most of the invited dowsers agreed on one

The Whispering Knights
In folklore, three knights were turned to stone by a witch. These stones still stand near the Rollright circle, where they once formed the sides of a burial chamber.

point. Almost all of them thought that there had been at least one other concentric circle of stones at Rollright. However, there is so far no proof for this claim.

Searching for energy

Many of the dowsers involved in the tests made claims about "energy" at the site that could not be verified. But Welsh dowser Bill Lewis did produce some phenomena that could not be accounted for.

For decades, he had reported dowsable areas of energy around standing stones. Lewis said this energy interacted with a stone at

> On a more accountable level, energy dowsers sometimes assist archeologists engaged in excavations to find specific features.

areas he called "nodes." In 1975, he was filmed dowsing a stone in Wales. Lewis pinpointed several of these nodes, which were then confirmed as natural magnetic anomalies by a physicist using a gaussmeter (a special scientific instrument that measures the strength of a magnetic field).

At Rollright, Lewis dowsed a node on the circle's tallest stone, and wired it up to a voltmeter, which gave steady positive readings. Then, Lewis, who is a healer as well as a dowser, leaned against the node as if performing a laying on of hands. The voltmeter's readings went haywire. No one else could reproduce this effect, yet Lewis produced it every time he tried.

The Dragon Project sometimes also employs an EEG (electroencephalograph) device called a "Mind Mirror." It is placed on dowsers while they work. The device showed characteristic "search mode" brain wave patterns in some dowsers, particularly Bill Lewis.

they believe in. Hence even at the same site, energy dowsers may find markedly different patterns of energy. A dowser who believes in the Hartmann grid, for example, will find squares of energy 6 1/2 feet by 8 feet, whereas an adherent of the Curry Net line system might find lines of energy 11 to 13 feet apart.

Divining the invisible

Despite all the confusion, however, there is little doubt that the dowsers believe they are getting a reaction that indicates *something* at these sites. Results of scientific tests would seem to bear out their beliefs. Some of the "energies" sensed at the stones appear to register as measurable physical forces on specialized scientific equipment.

At the Rollright stone circle in Britain, some of the points picked out by dowsers were shown to be "hot-spots" of natural radioactivity. At times these stones produced "flares" that were captured on infrared cameras. One energy dowser also picked out an apparent sevenfold circular pattern at the stone circle. This was claimed, during tests with a sensitive magnetometer, to correspond with a sevenfold spiral magnetic anomaly (a local variation in the earth's magnetic field). Although the dowsers identified the exact stones that produced these strange magnetic effects, no one knows why the effects occur.

How dowsing works

Why dowsers are able to respond to so many different types of earth energies is also a mystery. A number of intensive studies have been conducted by various scientists throughout this century in an

A ley with a view
Old Sarum, Salisbury cathedral, and Clearbury Ring can be seen lying in a straight line on this ley in Wiltshire, England.

effort to understand more about dowsing. These include one by Duane Chadwick of Utah State University in 1970 and another in the 1980's by Gene Simmons, a geophysicist from the Massachusetts Institute of Technology. It has been suggested that dowsers exhibit an exaggerated sensitivity to tiny changes in natural radiation and ionization, and magnetic electrostatic fields. But when the response was tested experimentally, it varied from one energy dowser to another, and was rarely consistent even with one dowser.

Physiologically, the dowser has a very strong, almost uncontrollable physical response that is similar to the knee-jerk reflex. But the dowser's response would appear to involve both body and mind — and dowsers themselves often claim that any energy, physical or psychic, can affect this response. The dowsing response appears to be most effective at discovering precise changes, and weakest at recognizing slow change. In a British test in 1908, 12 dowsers were unable to tell that they were standing over an underground reservoir, where water lay everywhere beneath them. Yet they had little trouble finding its *edge*, since that was a precise line of change.

Brain waves

Almost the only consistent feature of dowsers at work is a characteristic EEG (electroencephalograph) or brain wave pattern. Dowsers produce more of the brain waves associated with meditation or deep sleep. This may indicate that they are in touch with their environment on a deeper, subconscious level.

Dowsing is sometimes claimed to be a way of relearning the kind of intuitive awareness of the landscape that animals appear to have. Dowsers have shown that *something* special is occurring at ancient sites — though just what it is, and whether ancient peoples were consciously aware of it, remain to be discovered.

Space travelers
These pictographs from the Needles section of Canyonlands National Park in Utah are often cited as evidence that ancient peoples were once in contact with the occupants of UFO's. It has even been suggested that the aliens used energy from lines in the landscape to fuel their ships.

SEEING SPOTS

Dowsing for various earth energies has produced a mass of data that is very difficult to interpret. This confusion may have permitted energy dowsers to persuade themselves, and others, that they had found particular patterns of energy in some of the landscapes they have surveyed.

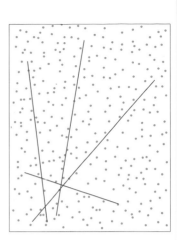

N O ONE IS SURE HOW, or even if, energy dowsing works. But some dowsers say that they are able to sense natural or paranormal energies in the environment and respond to them. While it may, at least conceivably, be possible that dowsers searching for earth energies can sense some or all of these forces at sites, the patterns of energy they perceive are likely to be highly subjective.

Dowsing for energy differs from dowsing for water, minerals, or other objects in that the latter three are tangible and their existence at a site can be proven. If a dowser identifies a specific area beneath the surface of the earth that he or she believes to contain certain minerals, for example, those minerals will either be found upon excavation or not. Mystical patterns of energy, however, are not only intangible — they may not exist!

Missing witnesses

A further problem confronts those searching for energy patterns: When dowsers search for water, minerals, lost objects, or oil, they use what is known as a "witness" — that is, a sample of what they are looking for. This witness can be fixed to the dowsing tool, held in the hand, or visualized by the dowser as a mental image. But since mystic energy patterns are not tangible, there are no samples to use as witnesses.

When dowsers search for something as general as earth energy, they are likely to pick up undifferentiated signals, into which they can read almost any energy pattern. Making sense of these random

patterns is a highly subjective process, so the individual energy dowser may consciously or unconsciously continue to find his or her own preferred pattern.

Dot-to-dot

The process of searching for mystic energy is simulated in the diagrams here.

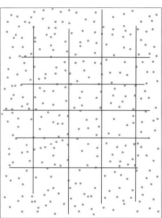

Each diagram has the same collection of randomly placed dots, representing the environment of undifferentiated energies in which an energy dowser claims to operate. The scale of each diagram could be that of a single site, or even a whole area of countryside.

It is all too easy to extract strikingly different patterns of energy from the same random collection of dots, as the examples here demonstrate. The lines, grids, crosses, and interweaving currents that are drawn over the dots are typical of the different types of energy patterns that various energy dowsers claim to have detected and mapped at a variety of different prehistoric sacred sites.

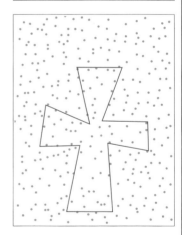

Unreliable method

Because dowsing for energies is so subjective, it is not a reliable method of learning about them. Until researchers know more about such earth energies, dowsing cannot be used to prove — or disprove — their existence.

> **When dowsers search for something as general as earth energy, they are likely to pick up undifferentiated signals, into which they can read almost any pattern.**

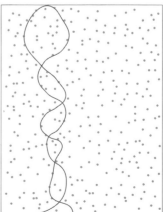

Dot matrix
The diagrams at right illustrate some of the many energy patterns that dowsers claim to have found at ancient sites.

At some healing wells, it was not
enough simply to drink the water
to effect a cure. The sick person
was also required to perform the
time-honored rituals that were
customary at that well. Some of
the wells, for example, were only
active on a certain day of the year,
or at a certain time. For example,
wells dedicated to St. John were
believed to cure ailments only on
the pagan festival of Midsummer.

Sometimes, the water had to be
used in special ways. In places
where total or partial immersion
was the custom, stone tanks with
steps leading into the water were
built. Elsewhere it was sufficient
simply to wash the affected area
or to drink the water. At other
wells, the water had to be drunk

Madron Well
*Madron Well, in Cornwall,
England, is one of the famous
"clootie" wells that are
widespread throughout Britain.*

from a special receptacle. Legend
has it that at the Whooping Cough
Well in Perth, Scotland, the water
had to be drunk from the horn of
a cow in order to be effective.

The ancient ritual of hanging a
piece of cloth on a nearby bush is
the custom at several holy wells.
People seeking physical or
spiritual relief still hang up pieces
of cloth, called clooties, near
these wells. The custom is a form
of sympathetic magic: according to
legend, the affliction leaves the
sufferer as the cloth decays.

WATER: SACRED AND STRANGE

*Water is a necessity for life and is treated
with great respect by most cultures
around the world. In myth and legend,
water is the magic liquid that can cure
any number of ills, promote immortality,
and even bring the dead back to life.*

IN ANCIENT TIMES, many civilizations considered
water to be sacred. Wherever rivers flowed,
springs welled up out of the ground, or waterfalls
rushed over rocks, some spiritual force was felt to be
present and was worshiped by all who visited. Prayers
and sacrifices were offered at these sacred places, and
people came to be cured of their ailments or
to seek answers to their problems.

Faith in the sacred qualities of water is
deep-seated in the human psyche. It survives
today in the belief in wishing wells and the
revitalizing powers of mineral spas.

Sacred sources

Apart from their life-giving properties, springs
and their man-made counterparts, wells,
have been considered since earliest times to
have special qualities. Some were associated
with gods, goddesses, saints, spirits, and even
demons. Many were said to have the power
to restore health — to clear the eyes, mend limbs, cure
diseases, and ease childbirth. Although the virtues of

> **Faith in the sacred qualities
> of water is deep-seated in the
> human psyche. It survives today in
> the belief in wishing wells
> and the revitalizing powers
> of mineral spas.**

the thermal springs at Bath in the west of England are
disregarded by conventional physicians today, their
mineral-rich waters still enjoy a reputation for being
able to alleviate rheumatism and diseases of the skin.
The waters were popular with the Romans, who built a
temple dedicated to Minerva, the goddess of wisdom,
there. At the site, archeologists have discovered altars
and carvings, as well as hundreds of lead tablets
inscribed with ancient prayers and curses. The people

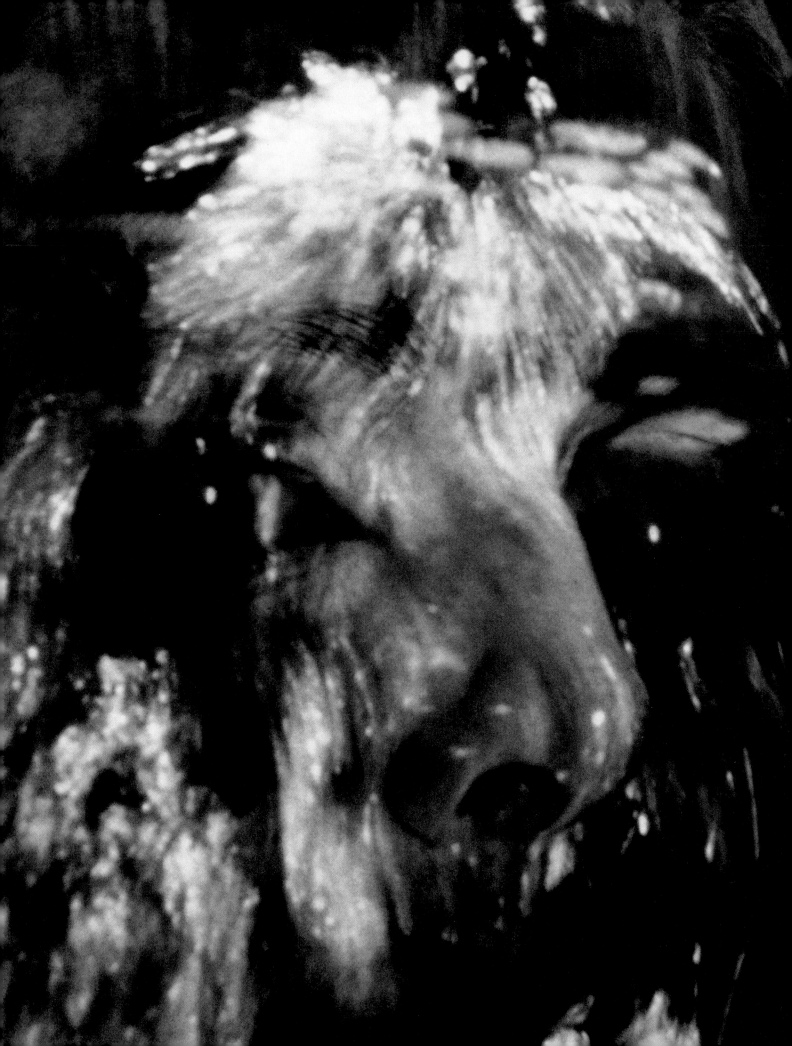

Many ancient holy wells now bear the names of Christian saints. Some of these wells were once pagan sacred springs.

St. Beuno's Well
Skulls or carved stone faces, like this one in Wales, are found at many ancient wells in northern Europe, perhaps signifying some lost form of cult practice, or indicating that the wells were once seen as oracles.

Precious water
The symbols of the water goddess, Chalchihuitlicue, who was thought to manifest herself in whirlpools, decorate this ornamental Aztec featherwork made in the late 15th century.

of every country in which such springs occur believe them to have special healing powers. After a widespread plague in Rome caused thousands of deaths in 3 B.C., a temple containing thermal springs dedicated to Asclepius, the god of healing, was established in an attempt to rid the land of disease. The temple was sited on a small island in the river Tiber, called Insula Tiberina, and remained a popular center of healing into medieval times. And thermal baths can still be found in some parts of Italy; the Aquae Termi baths in Alessandria, in the north of the country, are still in use.

Holy springs and wells are not as dramatic as megalithic monuments such as Stonehenge and Carnac in France. Yet sacred waters once played an important part in religious ritual. If modern dowsers are to be believed, water can be detected beneath almost all ancient sacred sites. When the British businessman Alfred Watkins, who coined the term leys, was researching ley lines in Britain in the 1920's, he claimed to find many holy wells and sacred springs along the alignments. Watkins also noted that churches were often built over or alongside holy or healing wells of ancient origin. In a similar sign of Britain's conversion to Christianity, many holy wells now bear the names of Christian saints. Some of these wells were once pagan sacred springs.

Holy springs and wells
Coventina's Well in Northumberland, England, was dedicated to Coventina, a local Celtic healing goddess adopted by the Romans. Discovered near a Roman temple, the well was found to contain a remarkable collection of offerings to the goddess: carved heads, over 20 altar

stones, figurines, jewelry, a skull, and more than 14,000 coins. The well was the principal temple of a cult dedicated to water nymphs, the elemental spirits of water who were thought to reside there.

Despite the coming of Christianity, local people often remained devoted to their pagan wells. In an effort to convert them, the wells were simply rededicated to a Christian saint, thereby giving them a new spiritual significance. In the 6th century, St. Brigid, abbess of Kildare, Ireland, became popular partly because she bore the same name as the Celtic goddess. Some of St. Brigid's holy wells may once have been dedicated to the goddess: one of these wells, in County Dublin, is now a Catholic shrine.

Saintly origins

Other holy wells were founded by early saints. The 7th-century medicinal well at Holywell, Wales, bears the name of St. Winifrid, who, according to legend, was decapitated by a spurned suitor. The severed head was later replaced by St. Beuno, who breathed new life into the girl. A strong spring burst out of the stony soil where the head had fallen.

Promoting fertility

In 1686, James II, king of England, visited the well with his second wife in an effort to ensure the birth of a son and heir to the throne after their first 10 children had died in infancy. A healthy son was born two years later. The well has continued to be a major pilgrimage center ever since. Even today, thousands of people visit it every year to drink its sacred water in the hope of curing their ailments.

Miraculous water
Water flowing from Mount Gatjan, in southern Serbia, is believed to cure diabetes and restore sight. Many claim to have been healed as soon as the water is poured into their eyes.

EXPERIMENTS ON WATER

Unlike most liquids, which contract as they cool and freeze, water contracts as it cools down to 38°F (4°C) and then expands as it freezes into the solid state. This explains why ice floats on the surface of lakes and ponds.

Ice itself is one of the most perfectly bonded structures known, with precise crystalline lattices that persist even when water returns to its liquid state, almost as if water retains a memory of its icy crystalline state.

Water memory

Whether or not water has some sort of memory has been the focus of several controversial experiments. In 1988, French immunologist Jacques Benveniste and his colleagues caused a furor within the scientific community when they claimed that they had observed white blood cells reacting to antibody solutions so dilute that there was no trace of the antibody molecules. They suggested that perhaps water "remembered" the structure of the antibody and could act as a "mold" for it, affecting white blood cells with which it was mixed.

Benveniste's theory would, if proven, explain why the scientifically derided practice of homeopathy works. (In homeopathy, extremely dilute solutions of substances that provoke certain diseases are said to be effective in

The waters of memory
One controversial theory suggests that the special qualities of water may be linked with the human brain's mysterious powers of memory.

treating those very diseases.) However, although Benveniste's work has been duplicated at laboratories in various countries throughout the world, his results remain highly controversial.

Water on the brain

In his paper *Water — Friend or Foe?* (1985), Dr. Cyril Smith of Salford University, England, claims that water can memorize the electrical frequencies to which it is exposed. And American physicist Fred Alan Wolf, writing in the book *Mind and the New Physics* (1984), suggests that water may even explain the mystery of the way memory is stored in the brain. He believes that microscopic drops of water present at the synapses (connections between brain cells) may help electrochemical signals to pass between the cells.

In the 1930's, German engineer Theodor Schwenk conducted experiments in which he shook a number of bottles of water before, during, and after a solar eclipse. When he germinated wheat grains in the bottles, he reported significant stunting in those grains that were germinated in the water shaken during the eclipse. He therefore concluded that water is a highly receptive medium "open to the cosmos."

The ability of specific geological factors to influence the human subconscious mind is the subject of a current Anglo-American research program for the Dragon Project (an enterprise run by earth mysteries enthusiasts who analyze prehistoric sites using specialized equipment). Four "dream sites" in Britain have been chosen for their interesting geophysical properties. Three of them are in Cornwall: the Chûn Quoit dolmen and the Carn Euny chambers, both of which have relatively high natural

Carn Euny
Preliminary analysis of dreams at Carn Euny, Cornwall, shows some evidence of common themes and images. This suggests that sacred places may play an active role in forming the content of dreams.

radiation levels, plus a Celtic holy well, whose water is found to be mildly radioactive. In Wales, a hill peak called Carn Ingli has been selected for its magnetic anomaly and earth light phenomena.

During the experiments each dream volunteer is accompanied on site by a helper, who watches carefully for rapid eye movements, or REMs. The flickering eyeballs beneath closed lids are indicative of dreaming. The helper wakes the volunteer during REM sleep, and any dreams he or she can recall are tape-recorded immediately. These recordings are later entered into a computer database. When enough dreams per site have been collected, they will be analyzed for similarities in dream imagery.

TEMPLES OF DREAM

One of the special powers of sacred places is their alleged ability to open the mind to waking visions and vivid dreams. Since ancient times, people have slept at sacred places in order to heal diseases, learn divination, or make contact with spirits.

*I*N THE SHINTO TEMPLE OF USA IN KYUSHI, ancient Japanese emperors would often sleep on a special polished stone bed, the *kamudoko*, in order to dream answers to problems of state. In India sleeping in temples to inspire dreams was a common practice and is still carried on to some extent today. Even in the Bible, dreams were linked with certain structures — Jacob reportedly dreamt of angels on a heavenly ladder as he slept with his head on a stone (Genesis 30:11–12). He built a temple at the site called Bethel.

Water was often associated with sacred sleep. Among the Celts of Britain, seers would wrap themselves in animal skins and lie near holy pools or waterfalls in order to have visionary dreams. In ancient Greece there were 320 documented dream temples, or Asclepions, all of which had sacred springs. Water played an important part in the purification procedures that were followed at these ancient dream temples.

The Greek dream temples were dedicated to the god of healing, Asclepius, who according to local legend was taught by the centaur Chiron to use a serpent to locate medicinal herbs and plants. The serpent, usually coiled around a rod, became one of the symbols associated with Asclepius. Since the Greeks believed that Asclepius effected cures or prescribed remedies in dreams, the practice of sleeping in temples dedicated to him became common.

A sick person would stay for a period at an Asclepion, making offerings and undergoing various purifications, such as bathing in, and drinking copious amounts of, the temple's sacred waters.

The temple of Apollo
Sleep healing was commonly practiced at this Asclepion on the Island of Cos. The columns mark the remains of the temple of Apollo.

Therapeutic sleep, or dream incubation, took place at the Asclepions, many of which are near mineral springs. Typically, a sick person would stay for a period at an Asclepion, making offerings and undergoing various purifications, such as bathing in, and drinking copious amounts of, the temple's sacred waters. Then the patient would fall asleep in a specialized cell called an *abaton*, hoping to dream of Asclepius or one of his symbols. Afterwards, a helper or *therapeute* — the word from which our term "therapy" derives — would assist the sufferer in analyzing the dream. The dream had to be interpreted to find out what cure was indicated. In some cases, the very act of dreaming at a temple had a healing effect.

Radiation and healing

One of the major Greek Asclepions was at ancient Corinth. Little now remains of the temple except, amazingly, some stone couches that have survived *in situ* in the abaton area. The temple contains a sacred fountain and water reservoirs. Greek archeologist Savas Kasas believes that the water was transported from the mineral-rich and mildly radioactive thermal springs at Loutraki, seven miles away, via an ancient road that linked the two sites. Although the ancients had no means of measuring radioactivity, it is possible that they recognized the healing powers of radioactive waters.

Some researchers have speculated that brief exposure to doses of mild natural radioactivity might promote healing by means of a homeopathic effect. At the old uranium mines of Boulder, Montana, people seeking cures for various ailments are exposed by experienced alternative medical therapists to strictly timed and very small doses of radon, a radioactive gas that is found in the uranium mines.

Research on radon gas

Research conducted at the University of Pittsburgh shows that some parts of the U.S.A. with high radon counts tend to have a lower incidence of certain kinds of cancer. Similar results have been obtained in Finland and Britain. But despite these findings, scientists believe that prolonged exposure to radioactive materials such as radon is harmful.

Dream temples were also used by the Romans, who built them in the farthest reaches of their empire. In Britain the remains of a fourth-century A.D. dream temple have been discovered at Lydney in Gloucestershire. This was dedicated to the British god of hunting and healing, Nodens, who was also associated with water.

The remains of the pagan temple complex stand on a promontory overlooking the River Severn, and overlie an iron mine. Is it merely accidental that the temple builders chose to place their site over extensive iron deposits? Perhaps not, for some archeologists have recently discovered the site of another dream temple in Thistleton, Leicestershire. That, too, stands over an ancient iron deposit. Perhaps this provides evidence that geological factors were indeed considered important at sites where altered mind states were of prime concern.

Epidauros
At many Asclepions, nonpoisonous snakes were kept as living symbols of the god. At the chief Asclepion, Epidauros, in Argolis, southern Greece, a snake pit, probably pre-dating the now ruined temple complex, still exists in one corner of the abaton. The pit stands near the well that held the temple's sacred waters.

God of sleep
This polished black obsidian mask discovered in Mexico City dates back to the 14th century. It is thought to represent Ixtilton, the Aztec god who visited children in their beds and brought them peaceful sleep.

CHAPTER TWO

ANCIENT LIGHT SHOWS

The mysteries of stone circles and other prehistoric monuments have long fascinated scientists and lay observers. Who built these earth shrines? What did they look like? And what was their purpose?

Many ancient sacred structures look out toward specific heavenly bodies, or face the sunrise or moonrise at certain times of the year. In some cases, they cast shadows that appear to have been part of some unknown ritual. And many experts now believe that the builders of these remarkable sites aligned them so that they might honor and perhaps interact with specific calendar events and astronomical phenomena. If true, this theory raises a number of questions: Why was so much time and energy lavished on building these structures? Who used them? What was the nature of the rituals that took place there?

Magic circle
The Stonehenge that visitors see today is the ruined remains of the last phase of building, which was completed over 3,500 years ago.

The first Stonehenge

The study of these intriguing questions, which requires the fusion of archeology and astronomy, is often referred to as archeoastronomy, or less commonly, astroarcheology. Such investigations began in earnest at the beginning of the 20th century with the detailed work of the eminent British astronomer Sir Norman Lockyer, who was also the editor of the science journal *Nature*. His research focused on Greek and Egyptian temples, which, Lockyer discovered, showed alignment with the sunrise and sunset. In more recent years, Alexander Thom, a retired professor of engineering at Oxford University, made perhaps the most important contribution to the field of archeoastronomy with his careful examination of sites all over Britain. Today, further research suggests that many other ancient sites, such as Carnac in northern France and Chichén Itzá in Central America, also exhibit complex astronomical alignments. The most famous archeoastronomic site in

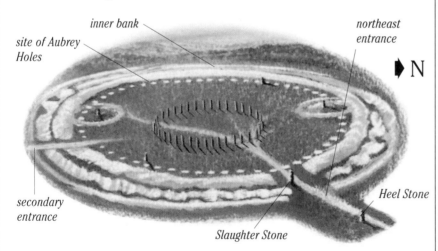

inner bank
site of Aubrey Holes
northeast entrance
▶ N
secondary entrance
Heel Stone
Slaughter Stone

the world, however, is undoubtedly the impressive megalithic monument known as Stonehenge, in Wiltshire, England.

The Stonehenge story
Contrary to long-standing belief, most experts now agree that Stonehenge was never an observatory where prehistoric astronomers surveyed the skies. It has always been a temple, and superstition —

not science — probably dominated the minds of its ancient builders. Another myth concerning the famous structure is that Stonehenge was originally a Druid site. It was not, for we now know that it had been standing for thousands of years before the heyday of the Druids.

Although it may strike observers as a stone symbol of strength and stability, the circle has changed dramatically since it was originally erected over 5,000 years ago. The changes probably took place in three main phases of construction.

The first Stonehenge
About 3200 B.C., experts believe that the farming families of Salisbury Plain in southern England dug out the ditch of a wide, circular earthwork known as a henge. The structure had an inner bank broken only by two entrances, one 35 feet wide at the northeast, and a second, narrower one set accurately at the south. The ancient diggers probably located south by establishing the midpoint between midwinter sunrise and sunset.

This earth shrine was aligned to the moon. Evidence of the moon's role was uncovered in 1923 by British antiquarian William Hawley. While excavating the causeway of the northeastern entrance, he came upon six lines of holes where 53 closely set posts had once stood. Hawley could not explain their presence, since if they had all been erected together, they would have blocked this entrance to the earthwork. The mystery was solved in 1963, when C. A. Newham, a retired Gas Board official, discovered that the posts charted the movements of the moon.

The movements of the moon
In contrast to the sun, the moon does not always rise in exactly the same position on the horizon on the same day of the year. The moon does not follow a yearly cycle, but instead revolves around the earth about 12 times a year. (Because the earth revolves around the sun once a year, the sun rises and sets at exactly the same place on the same day every year.) Viewed from the earth, the moon itself completes an arc between the extreme points at which it rises every 18.6 years.

Each year the prehistoric observers erected a post in line with the position in the northeast where the moon rose in midwinter. This was recorded over six long cycles — a period of over a century.

At the end of this period, the ancient observers were able to locate accurately the position of the most northerly rising of the moon, to which they aligned one side of the northeast entrance to the monument. This entrance was laid out as a "window," the other side of which was aligned to the midpoint of the arc of the moon. To mark these lines, pairs of tall standing stones were set up at the outer edges of the causeway — to the east of it, the alignment to the middle of the lunar cycle was defined by the presence of the now-fallen Slaughter Stone and the Heel Stone beyond it. At the western side of the entrance, two high pillars stood in line with the point of the most northerly moonrise. Once the role of the moon is

---

Stonehenge has always been a temple, and superstition — not science — probably dominated the minds of its builders.

---

understood, it is clear that, contrary to popular belief, the remaining Heel Stone never pointed to a midsummer sunrise, since it was 20 feet too far to the east.

Death's dominion

The ancient builders of Stonehenge were obsessed with the activity of the moon because for them the moon was linked with death. For over a thousand years, the ancestors of these people had buried their dead in enormous earthen barrows, whose long mounds pointed toward the moon between its northern (midwinter) and southern (midsummer) risings. At Stonehenge the lunar alignment was more precisely charted, perhaps because the society had become more complex.

At the center of this first construction of Stonehenge stood a 100-foot wide ring of posts, possibly a freestanding circle, experts speculate, but probably a roofed mortuary where the bodies of the dead would be laid out on the floor until they had decomposed. This practice was common in Neolithic Britain. In ditches at the ends of both entrances, Hawley

found the bones of children and adults. It is possible that these were sacrificial victims whose deaths may have been thought to give power to the earthwork.

After several centuries the timber structure decayed and different customs apparently developed. Around 2400 B.C.,

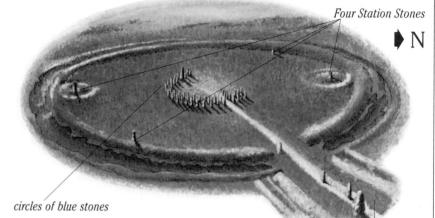

The second Stonehenge

Four Station Stones

▶ N

circles of blue stones

widened entrance

investigators suggest, users of poorly fired pottery vessels known as Grooved Ware dug out a ring of 56 pits about three feet wide inside the bank; these are called the Aubrey Holes, after John Aubrey, who discovered them in 1666. At significant locations — on the main axis, at the two entrances, and at the extreme east and south — cremated human remains, balls of chalk, newly shed antlers, and broken pottery were found. Smaller holes inside the bank held tiny deposits of burnt bone. In one of these a small, beautifully polished mace head was buried. This object must have been important to the Grooved Ware cult, for it seems to have been placed in alignment with the most southerly rising of the moon, apparently linking it with the moon as well as death.

The second Stonehenge

The next major change in the structure of Stonehenge occurred about 200 years later, around 2200 B.C., with the emergence of a new people. Archeologists call this new society the Beaker people,

Polished amulet
Discovered in a small hole inside the bank, this mace head is made of a stripy rock called hornblendic gneiss, which is found in Scotland and France.

ASTRONOMICAL TERMS
Solstices
The summer solstice occurs on the longest day of the year, when the sun rises and then sets at its most northerly position on the horizon. This is usually about June 21.

The winter solstice occurs on the shortest day of the year, when the sun rises and then sets at its most southerly position. This is usually about December 21.

Equinoxes
Every year the vernal equinox falls on or about March 21, while the autumnal equinox falls on or about September 21. At both these times, the sun rises and sets due east and west, and the days and nights are of equal length.

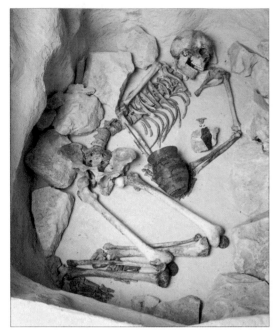

Beaker burial
This grave dates from the period when the blue stones were brought to Stonehenge, about 2200 B.C. Buried with the occupant were a typical pottery drinking vessel and a bronze dagger.

Ancient weapon
Similar to the one in the Beaker grave (above), this bronze dagger has been given a replica shaft.

after the brightly colored, geometrically patterned earthenware drinking vessels often found in their graves. The Beaker people may have been immigrants who crossed the North Sea, or local people who developed new ideas and ways of doing things. They made dramatic alterations to Stonehenge, transforming the site into a temple of the sun, rather than the moon. Evidence suggests that these people were sun worshipers: Thin gold discs incised with simple sunlike motifs have been discovered under their round earthen burial mounds, or barrows.

The Beaker people remodeled the site radically, setting up two concentric but incomplete stone circles at the center. These circles were made from about 80 huge blue stones, up to about seven tons in weight, from the Preseli mountains of southwest Wales, over 200 miles away. It was once thought that the blue stones had been transported across water and land by the builders of Stonehenge especially for this purpose, but the discovery of a similar stone in a nearby earthen barrow, which had been abandoned about 1,000 years before the Stonehenge circle was built, suggests that the massive blue stones might have been deposited by glaciers in the area.

The line of the solstice
The Beaker people changed the main axis of the henge by throwing 25 feet of the bank back into the ditch, thus widening the northeast entrance to the right. This caused the axis to swing from 46° to 50° from the north/ south line. The middle of this wider entrance was now in direct alignment with the sunrise at the summer solstice. (This made the remaining Heel Stone appear central to the entrance, an illusion that has misled numerous people attempting to unravel the mystery of Stonehenge. It was, in fact, still slightly to one side.) The banks on either side of the avenue were then extended down to the River Avon.

The Four Station Stones
The Beaker people also added a large rectangle around the stone circles, with stones marking the corners. Called the Four Stations, only two survive; one has fallen and the other is a battered stump. The long sides of the rectangle extended some 262 feet northwest by southeast, the short sides about 110 feet northeast by southwest. Lines drawn through the rectangle's short sides seem to frame the midsummer sunrise, while the long sides define the most northerly position of the setting moon. A diagonal running from east-southeast to west-northwest pointed toward sunset on May Day, the Celtic festival of Beltine, the "Shining One." Some researchers believe that the Four Station Stones were erected at an earlier stage, during the construction of the first stone circle at Stonehenge. Evidence to support this theory remains largely inconclusive, but experts agree that they were certainly present in the second Stonehenge.

The third Stonehenge
Further changes followed the flowering of the Early Bronze Age, around 2000 B.C. The area around Stonehenge became a huge cemetery filled with round barrows that covered the graves of chieftains and their women. These barrows contained articles made of bronze, copper, amber, gold, and a primitive glass called faience. Stonehenge became more imposing, a monument befitting the status of the people buried in the barrows nearby.

First, the blue stones were replaced with massive sarsen (sandstone) blocks dragged from the Marlborough Downs 20 miles away. These were carefully shaped and erected in the circle. Experts now know exactly what this looked like, but

> Stonehenge had changed from a communal place of worship into a site serving an elite priestly cult.

the precise significance of its form is still a mystery. The main ring consisted of 30 upright stones supporting 30 lintels that were linked continuously around the top. Inside the ring, in a huge horseshoe shape, were five enormous three-stone arches, or trilithons, each consisting of two pillars supporting a lintel. At the center of the curve of the inner ring an exceptionally large single stone, known as the Altar Stone, stood upright like a pillar. It is now buried beneath larger fallen stones.

Transformation of Stonehenge

The main axis of Stonehenge was now reversed. The horseshoe was open to the northeast, but became gradually taller in the direction of the largest trilithon to the southwest. This is where the sun set at midwinter. Culturally, the change was even more dramatic. Not only had the monument been transformed from a temple of the moon to a center for sun-worship, it had also been changed from a communal place of worship into a sacred site serving an elite priestly cult.

Cult of the dead

Even in its last years of use, Stonehenge preserved links with its previous, popular incarnation. It was never an interest in

The third Stonehenge

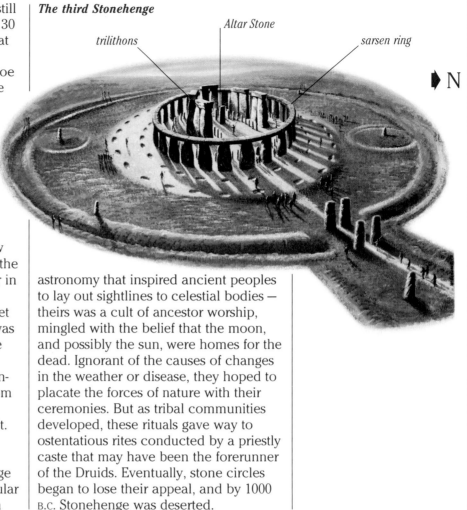

trilithons   Altar Stone   sarsen ring

▶ N

astronomy that inspired ancient peoples to lay out sightlines to celestial bodies — theirs was a cult of ancestor worship, mingled with the belief that the moon, and possibly the sun, were homes for the dead. Ignorant of the causes of changes in the weather or disease, they hoped to placate the forces of nature with their ceremonies. But as tribal communities developed, these rituals gave way to ostentatious rites conducted by a priestly caste that may have been the forerunner of the Druids. Eventually, stone circles began to lose their appeal, and by 1000 B.C. Stonehenge was deserted.

THE MARRIAGE OF THE GODS

One new piece of research suggests that the third phase of Stonehenge might have been built to celebrate the annual marriage of the Great Goddess and the Sky God. In his 1992 book *The Stonehenge Solution*, Prof. G. T. Meaden, Oxford physicist and antiquarian, describes how the consummation of this celestial marriage was enacted ritually by the play of light and shade around the massive standing stones.

Sign of the Sky God

According to Prof. Meaden's theory, the horseshoe arrangement of the inner-sanctum stones represented the womb of the goddess. In order to reach it, the sun's rays at the summer solstice had to pass the Heel Stone, which had been deliberately positioned slightly to the east of the avenue, outside the monument (seen as the body of the goddess). Immediately after an unobstructed sunrise, the Heel Stone eclipsed the sun, forming a shadow that symbolized the phallus of the Sky God. The long shadow entered the central archway of the main sarsen ring and eventually reached the Altar Stone,

Consummate spectacle
As the sun rises in the sky, the shadow of the Heel Stone retreats from the ring.

which, in the context of Meaden's theory, might more accurately be called the Egg Stone or Goddess Stone. Particles of shiny mica embedded in this large rock caused it to glint in the morning sun; the moment of climax occurred when the phallic shadow formation extinguished its light. The retreat of the shadow represented withdrawal, and this too was a part of the spectacle watched by hundreds of people from outside the monument at the summer solstice.

Symbolic shadow

Prof. Meaden's theory is supported by the fact that in many primitive religions, goddess and god conceived perpetually to symbolize the renewal of the earth, and to provide reassurance that the universe, as the ancient worshipers knew and understood it, was secure. Despite the semi-ruined condition of Stonehenge, Meaden maintains that on the few days around the summer solstice, visitors can still witness the fertility spectacle that he believes lies behind its construction.

MEDIEVAL SYMBOLIC ASTRONOMY

Intricate, meaningful, and eye-catching light effects were a feature of many medieval Christian churches. In many cases, these churches occupied ancient pagan and Neolithic sacred sites.

THE SACRED SITES OF PREHISTORY are not the only places where astronomy was an integral part of religious ritual and ceremony. There are many examples of this link in medieval Christian buildings as well. What we may never know is whether this was a direct continuation of ancient pagan practices, or a reflection of medieval church builders' tendency to re-package the old religion for new symbolic purposes, such as attracting converts to Christianity.

A typical example of the use of astronomy in sacred architecture is the rock-hewn chapel atop a limestone pinnacle known as the Externsteine, near Detmold in Germany. Early Christian at the latest, the chapel may even be pagan in origin; today it is roofless and semiderelict, but still in place is a circular window that faces the position of the morning sun at the summer solstice. The window is situated above a pedestal, or altar, which according to German researcher William Teudt (1860–1942) may once have held a gnomon — a vertical stick or rod intended to cast a shadow. Teudt believed that on Midsummer Day, the rays of the rising sun entered through the chapel's circular window and penetrated the interior darkness so that the shadow cast by the gnomon fell directly into a niche on the opposite wall. The symbolism of this niche, or what it may have contained at one time, has long been forgotten.

Sacred spring

Also in Germany, at Aachen, is a spring that has been considered sacred since Celtic and Roman times. In the eighth century the Emperor Charlemagne made this site the capital of his empire. An octagonal palace chapel was built at the site under the careful supervision of an English monk named Alcuin, and the emperor gathered around him a cosmopolitan court with the aim of reconstituting the arts and sciences of antiquity. In the late 1970's a German photographer called Hermann Weisweiler uncovered evidence of the apparent influence of astronomy in the construction of the palace chapel. What he discovered was that at the summer solstice the sun's rays directly illuminated the sphere from which a Barbarossa Chandelier was suspended. He also found that Charlemagne's throne in the upper gallery was carefully positioned so that it is illuminated by the sun's rays on his birthday, April 16, at the summer solstice, and on both of the equinoxes. Furthermore, the photographer claimed that the floor plan of the chapel not only shows startling similarities to the layout of the Stonehenge circle (which is located on almost the same latitude), but is also the same size. One possible explanation for such an extraordinary parallel is that Alcuin brought the precise details of the design of Stonehenge with him to the palace chapel at Aachen.

> **Charlemagne's throne in the upper gallery was carefully positioned so that it is illuminated by the sun's rays on his birthday.**

A similar effect occurs at a 15th-century church in the alpine village of Elm, in Switzerland. Towering over the church is a mountain called the Tschingelhorner, in which there is a natural rock tunnel called St. Martin's Hole. Around the time of the equinoxes in March and September, the rays of the rising sun shine through this hole to illuminate the church tower over three miles away. Clearly, Elm church was deliberately positioned to take advantage of the light in this way, and some researchers think it was built on the site of a prehistoric structure that had also made use of the natural illumination. But while remains of Bronze Age structures have been found near the church, there is no evidence to support this theory.

Shining symbol

At the 13th-century Chartres cathedral in France there is perhaps the most famous example of medieval Christian symbolic astronomy in existence. Here, at noon on the summer solstice, the sun's rays shine through a clear pane in one of the stained-glass windows. The rays fall onto a small brass plate set in a paving stone in the transept's western aisle; this stone is not only larger than those around it, but is also of a different hue, and is set at an angle. Such an effect must have been deliberate, since it would have required the careful and planned cooperation of a variety of skilled people — architect, stonemason, and glazier — all working to detailed and accurate

astronomical information. A simpler example of possible medieval symbolic astronomy occurs at Rames Head, England, where the 14th-century chapel of St. Michael sits on a conical hill. The tiny chapel faces out to sea toward another conical rock called the Mewstones, which juts out of the water five miles away. Viewed from the chapel, the sun rises directly behind the Mewstones on St. Michael's Day, September 29.

From the evidence, it seems that the medieval builders might have been capable of including long landscape alignments in their astronomical schemes, as were the prehistoric builders of standing stone formations like Stonehenge. French researchers have found that the axis of the cathedral at St. Lizier is what is often known as equinoctial, in that it follows the line of the sunrise on March 21 and September 21. Also, the cathedral itself lies on what may be another significant astronomical alignment. This alignment runs from the point on Mont Redon four miles to the northwest, where the sun is known to rise at midwinter, to an ancient chapel at Marsan, half a mile to the southeast of the cathedral at St. Lizier.

The mystery of Chartres
This window at Chartres cathedral is dedicated to St. Apollinaire. At noon on Midsummer Day the rays of the sun shine through a clear pane in it to illuminate a small brass plate on the cathedral floor. Like many churches, Chartres stands on a pagan site, which in turn may have replaced an even older Neolithic holy place.

CELESTIAL SIGHTLINES

The discipline of archeoastronomy has revealed that some ancient sites are meant to be viewed in association with the sky and surrounding landscape. Many ancient peoples took advantage of natural horizon features, building their own sites from which to monitor celestial events.

*I*N THE AMERICAN SOUTHWEST the winter sky is crisp and clear. The sun has not yet risen, but the Anasazi sun priest in Chaco Canyon, New Mexico, can see the rimrock (the lip of the canyon) silhouetted against the dawn glow. He is looking across a small side canyon near the ancient Indian settlement now known as Wijiji. As the minutes pass, the growing light of the rising sun illuminates the landscape. Finally, the sun itself appears. From the narrow ledge on which he is standing, the sun priest sees only a section of the sun's outer rim, since most of it is blocked by the top of a sandstone pillar across the canyon. This natural feature marks the position of the winter solstice sunrise.

The changing year

The Anasazi sun priest knows that the year has reached a turning point. From now on, the sunrise will gradually slip farther north as spring approaches. Eventually it will reach its northern limit (June 21 in our calendar — the summer solstice). Then the gradual shift south will

The growing light of the rising sun illuminates the landscape. Finally, the sun itself appears.

begin again, and by this time next year (December 21 or so), the sun priest will return to his special place on the ledge to watch the winter sun. His vigil gives him vital reassurance about the continuing orderly passage of time and the seasons throughout the year.

According to the American astronomer E. C. Krupp, in his 1983 book, *Echoes of the Ancient Skies*, the astronomy of the ancients relied on two things only — a place to stand (backsight) and a point to look toward (foresight). In this case, the Wijiji ledge is the place to stand. It seems to have been selected as a backsight because it lines up the winter solstice sunrise with the foresight, which is the rimrock, 1,500 feet away to the southeast. We might not suspect that there was any astronomical significance in the Wijiji ledge if it were not marked by a fascinating array of rock paintings on the cliff wall and intricate carvings on the boulders. Some of the designs suggest an ancient Indian origin,

The moon at Callanish
The moon at its extreme southerly position in the 18.6-year lunar calendar, photographed in June 1987 at Callanish on the Isle of Lewis in Scotland. Viewed from the Callanish stone circle at this time, it can be seen to pass over a gap in the Harris Hills.

including a white sun disc and a dotted line that appears to point in the general direction of the rimrock foresight.

Yellow Jacket

In 1986, American astronomer J. McKim Malville and his colleague Mark Neupert identified an equally compelling Anasazi sightline at the ruins at Yellow Jacket, in southwestern Colorado, near Cortez. At least four shaped standing stones, one of which is still upright, and a cliffside shrine almost 600 feet farther northeast, established a line that continued to the horizon and targeted the sunrise at the summer solstice on the south slope of Mount Wilson, a prominent peak about 46 miles away. A distinctive needle of rock known as Lizard Head, just south of Mount Wilson, marks the position of the sun about 16 days before the summer solstice. Like the Wijiji ledge, it permits the observer to anticipate the time when the sun will reach its limit.

Although Wijiji and Yellow Jacket may appear to be dramatic examples of celestial sightlines, there is no written or oral record to confirm their purpose.

American Indian sightlines

Evidence of celestial sightlines survives, too, at the Mississippian site of Cahokia, southern Illinois, an enormous complex of ancient earthworks. Cahokia is made up of more than 100 mounds, most of which are oriented to the four cardinal directions. Archeologist Warren Wittry has revealed post holes in the complex that seem to form part of a circle. He suggests that giant posts were placed in a ring, a "sun circle," and that a sun priest watched astronomical events from the center. Wittry reconstructed some posts and confirmed by direct observation from the center of the circle that one post indicates equinox sunrise over the largest mound and the others mark the midsummer and midwinter sunrises.

Far to the south, in Central America, are the archeological remains of many ancient Indian cultures, some of which show evidence of connections with astronomy. One of the oldest examples comes from the ruins of Alta Vista, built in about A.D. 400 by the Chalchihuite Indians, near Zacatecas, Mexico. An observer at the solar temple at Alta Vista sees the sun at the equinoxes rise over Picacho Peak, about nine miles away. Alta Vista is about 400 miles from Mexico City and is apparently deliberately close to the tropic of Cancer, the latitude in

> **Giant posts were placed in a ring, a "sun circle," and a sun priest watched astronomical events from the center.**

which the sun passes directly overhead at noon on the summer solstice. About six miles to the south of Alta Vista is a high plateau known as Cerro El Chapin. At its summit is a flat rock on which are carved quartered double circles. From here, an observer can see the sunrise at the summer solstice over Picacho Peak. Similar circles are found at other sites and these may have been used to orient particular structures according to their astronomical alignment.

Looking for Venus

Venus, which is the brightest object in the sky apart from the sun and the moon, played a major role in the astronomies of the Central American Indians, particularly the Mayas. Its astronomical importance is evident at a Mayan ceremonial center called the Caracol, which consists of a cylindrical tower on a rectangular platform, built around A.D. 1000 at Chichén Itzá in the

The Maori sky god
The Maoris of New Zealand believe that horizon solstice points are the head (south) and feet (north) of Rangi, the sky god. This ancient Maori war-canoe prow represents the separation of the Earth Mother, Papa, from the Sky Father, Rangi. The spirals represent light and knowledge coming into the world.

Yucatán Peninsula, Mexico. Dr. Anthony Aveni, associate professor of astronomy at Colgate University, Hamilton, New York, and Professor Horst Hartung of the University of Guadalajara in Mexico, carried out a lengthy, detailed examination of the architecture of the Caracol and found that a number of small openings in the wall at the top of the tower are nearly aligned with the most extreme northerly and southerly setting points of Venus.

The Palace of the Governor at Uxmal

Another Mayan site in the Yucatán that aligns with Venus is the large complex known as Uxmal, which is a collection of open plazas with elevated buildings and tall, massive pyramids, all ornamented with Mayan Venus symbols. This large, impressive complex faces in the direction of the southernmost rising of Venus and frames an altar that is also aligned with the planet. This alignment reportedly continues three miles farther to the huge pyramid at Cehtzuc, which according to Aveni, marks the exact spot where Venus rose at its southernmost extension in the seventh century A.D.

Ancient European sites

In the 1960's, a British professor of engineering, Alexander Thom, and his colleagues surveyed hundreds of ancient sites in Britain and France. Some of the sites, they judged, may have served as celestial sightlines. At Ballochroy, on the west coast of Scotland, for example, are three slablike stones arranged in a line. Thom found that the orientation of the line toward the southwest passed over a cairn and indicated a midwinter setting sun behind one end of Cara Island, a few miles out to sea. Another sightline was found at Brittany in France. Here, Thom suggested that Le Grand Menhir Brisé, an enormous broken stone near the town of Locmariaquer had, when upright, acted as a foresight for lunar observations from positions all around nearby Quiberon Bay. However, this has been attacked by many statisticians, who point out that there are so many sites around Quiberon Bay that some backsights could occur on the appropriate sightlines quite by chance.

Long-distance alignments

Long-distance sun alignments are also found in Peru, India, and Polynesia. In Peru, the Incas built towers on the horizon at many sites to mark significant positions of the rising sun in the agricultural and ritual cycle. In Vijayangara, the 14th-century capital of medieval India, the Hundred Column Audience Hall formed the backsight for a summer solstice sunrise a mile away above a sacred hill. On Easter Island in the South Pacific a temple sits on the rim of a large crater called Rano Kau. From this temple, the sun rises at the summer solstice over Poike Peak, about 13 miles away at the northeast tip of the island.

EGYPTIAN HORIZONS

Since Alexander Thom proposed his candidates for ancient horizon astronomy, examples of celestial sightlines have been found all over the world. American Egyptologist Mark Lehner believes that the pyramid builders of Egypt made a horizon symbol out of the pyramids at Giza. From a position near the Sphinx, the summer solstice sun appears to set in the gap formed by the silhouettes of the Great Pyramid of Khufu and the Pyramid of Khafre.

The *Akhat*

These two pyramids and the space between them create the shape of the *akhat*, the Egyptian symbol for the mountain horizon. Through 3,000 years of Egyptian history, this hieroglyphic symbol is often drawn with the sun's huge disc lodged in the emblematic mountain notch. According to Zahi Hawass, an Egyptian Egyptologist, the name given to the Great Pyramid, *Akhet Khuru*, may also have meant "horizon of the sun."

The Caracol

The tower of the Caracol ceremonial center at Chichén Itzá shows almost perfect alignment with the setting position of Venus.

MAGICAL LIGHT AND SHADE

In many cultures throughout the world, the prehistoric builders designed and constructed their sacred monuments with great care to create dramatic lighting effects and shadow formations.

*M*ANY ANCIENT TEMPLES AND MONUMENTS were not observatories, as early researchers believed, but were constructed in order to incorporate astronomical phenomena into ceremonial activities. Ancient peoples "brought in" light — the power of the sun, moon, and perhaps planets — to sacred spaces. These spectacular sources of light and the shadows cast by them were used not only for ritual purposes but also, it would seem, for sheer sensational effect.

A good example of light shows within monuments is found at Burro Flats in the Simi Hills, Los Angeles. The flats contain an array of Chumash Indian rock paintings. The paintings depict centipedelike creatures, winged human forms, concentric rings, and handprints, which were a sign of sanctity in ancient times.

The magic of sunlight

The paintings at Burro Flats are sheltered by rocks for most of the year. But at midwinter the rising sun shines through a natural split in the rocks surrounding the shrine and unleashes a finger of light that illuminates the paintings. At the time of the winter solstice, the Chumash shaman, who watched the sun and kept the

Ancient peoples "brought in" the power of the sun, moon, and perhaps planets to sacred spaces.

calendar, would retire to the caves to witness the event. This visual phenomenon is thought to have been used, in conjunction with special hallucinogenic substances, to alter the state of consciousness of the shaman and produce a profound spiritual experience.

A similar ritual may also have been performed by Anasazi Indians at the great ritual kiva (a circular ceremonial structure) called Casa Rinconada, at Chaco Canyon, New Mexico, which is aligned with the four cardinal directions. At the summer solstice the rising sun pierces a hole in the kiva wall and illuminates one of six irregularly spaced niches in the opposite wall. There is some debate about the meaning of this, but it is suggested that the kiva might have been used as a ceremonial center. Casa Rinconada was located across

Casa Rinconada
Inside the great kiva Casa Rinconada, at Chaco Canyon, at the summer solstice sunrise, a beam of light passes through an aperture in the wall and falls directly on a niche in the opposite wall (above).

Sun symbols
At Cairn T, the chambered and intricately carved cairn on one of the Loughcrew Hills, near Newgrange in Ireland, a rectangle of dazzling sunlight spears into the mound on the day of the equinox, exactly framing an eight-rayed sun symbol carved on a stone in the back of the chamber.

Tomb lights
At the Newgrange burial mound in Ireland, the rising midwinter sun sends its beams through a special opening above the entrance, creating a shaft of light inside the darkened interior.

Rock paintings
At the Burro Flats, Los Angeles, the winter solstice sunrise sends a beam of light onto concentric rings painted on the walls of the shrine.

Chaco Canyon from Pueblo Bonito, a massive stone apartment complex where up to 60,000 people once lived. Sunlight may also have formed an integral part of the rituals and ceremonial activities that were performed at Isleta Pueblo, south of Albuquerque, New Mexico, where corn was reportedly "blessed" by the golden rays of the rising sun admitted at midday into the dark interior of the ceremonial room.

Magical tombs
It is still uncertain how the great Neolithic chambered mounds of Europe were used, but similar effects occur at some of them, and perhaps most spectacularly at a complex of monuments in the Boyne Valley, Ireland. The most famous of these is the vast burial mound, Newgrange, which dates from around 3000 B.C. There, on the winter solstice, the rays of the rising sun pierce an aperture above the entrance to the chamber. This creates a shaft of light that passes through the 60-foot passage and lights up the far end of the chamber. This phenomenon was long discounted as mere folklore, but in 1969 it was witnessed for the first time by the Irish archeologist, Michael O'Kelly, of University College, Cork. The debate as to whether the dramatic lighting effect was accidental was apparently settled in 1989 by Tom Ray, an astronomer at the

Dublin Institute for Advanced Studies, who was able to prove statistically that the burial mound had been deliberately designed so that this light phenomenon occurred only on the winter solstice.

An American artist and researcher, Martin Brennan, has since made further discoveries. He spent a decade studying the rock artwork of these and other Irish Neolithic monuments. He discovered that the entrance stone at Newgrange had a prominent vertical groove, which he suggested might have been an ancient glyph indicating the alignment of the sun at midwinter. On the opposite side of the tomb Brennan discovered another stone with vertical grooves. Both these stones lie along the line the sunbeam travels through the burial mound at midwinter.

In his book *The Stars and the Stones* (1983), Brennan writes about the lighting effects at Newgrange's companion burial mounds, Knowth and Dowth. One of the largest mounds of its kind, Knowth has two passages facing east and west. The

> ## At Newgrange, on the winter solstice, a shaft of light passes through the 60-foot passage and lights up the far end of the chamber.

entrance stones at both are marked with vertical grooves. The setting equinoctial sun sends a narrow beam down the west passage, which Brennan has described as "one of the great wonders of the ancient Neolithic world." At Dowth, the setting midwinter sun projects its light into the mound and is reflected off certain stones, producing a stunning light show. Effects like these have led many researchers to believe that the mounds were not merely tombs, but major ceremonial centers.

Landscape connections
At some ancient sacred sites, dramatic lighting effects are coupled with specific landscape alignments, suggesting that these prehistoric monuments might have been oriented on an astronomical basis. A clear example occurs at Maes Howe, a

large chambered mound in the Scottish Orkney islands. The mound appears to align with the midwinter sunset. At such times the disappearing sun sends golden rays down the long entrance passage to illuminate the dark inner chamber. The axis of this entrance passage, extended out into the surrounding countryside, strikes a massive standing stone called Barnhouse, which is in turn aligned with another single standing stone called the Watchstone, and a stone circle.

Solar and lunar effects

Various researchers have noticed that sunlight is not the only source for the amazing light shows at ancient sites. At Gavrinis in Brittany, a unique quartz

Sun daggers
A dagger of sunlight pierces through huge uprights, illuminating ancient carvings at the Tregastel tomb in Brittany, France.

block stands at a position in the passage where the beams from the midwinter sunrise intersect those from the moon at a key point in the 18.6-year lunar cycle. This large block is the only undecorated stone at the ancient site, and British archeologist Aubrey Burl has suggested that the quartz was deliberately placed to glow white when the sunbeams and moonbeams fell on it simultaneously.

The ruins of Karnak temple
The majestic temple of Karnak is now in ruins. It is the opinion of expert astronomers that the 3,000-year-old temple was built to align with the summer solstice sunset.

TEMPLES OF LIGHT

The evidence suggests that light-beam astronomy was used at temples throughout the world. It seems that ancient peoples knew how to take advantage of specific solar and lunar events in their religious and ceremonial activities.

IN THE 1890's the astronomer Norman Lockyer proved to his own satisfaction that Egyptian temples were aligned with sunrise and sunset at key times of the year. He noted that the temple at Karnak had a main axis that pointed to sunset at the summer solstice, and he pictured the sun's dying rays reaching in to illuminate the image of the god in the deep, dark sanctuary, lying directly on the axis.

However, in 1891, P. Wakefield, a British Army engineer, showed that hills located on the western horizon meant that to observe the sunset, a person would have to have been in a second-story room in the temple. There is no evidence of such a structure.

In 1973, astronomer Gerald Hawkins, at the Smithsonian Institution in Washington, D.C., published his findings, based on sophisticated calculations, temple hieroglyphics, and direct observations. It was his view that the axis was in fact intended to work in the other direction, toward the midsummer sunrise.

The Torreon

Another example of the use of sunbeams occurs at the Torreon temple in the famous Inca citadel of Machupicchu, Peru. In 1980, American astrophysicist David Dearborn discovered that the northeastern window of the inner sanctum of this now-roofless temple was directed at the midwinter sunrise. Beneath this window is an altarlike rock, which has been carved so that a sharp, regular cleft divides it in half and lies at right angles to the window.

When the solstitial sun rises above the San Gabriel Peak to the northeast, its light floods through the window, falling parallel to the rock cleft. Dearborn and American astronomer Ray White have proposed that a frame may have once hung on carved knobs that protrude from the wall in the Torreon, supporting a plumb line that would have thrown a shadow along the cut edge on the carved altar stone at the precise date of the solstice. We can only speculate as to the reason for such use of light-beam astronomy in ancient ceremonial activities.

The sun not only gives light, it casts shadows, and this effect was used by some prehistoric peoples in their religious and ceremonial astronomy.

Many of the Pueblo Indians of the American Southwest practiced sun-watching in their daily life, and watching shadows cast by the sun was an integral part of this tradition. Frank Cushing, an anthropologist with the Smithsonian Institution in Washington D.C., lived in Zuni Pueblo, New Mexico, for five years in the 1890's and observed the actions of the Zuni sun-watching priest there.

Sacred shadow play

One February morning Cushing followed the priest along a trail to the shrine of Matsaki. There, the priest slowly approached an open tower and seated himself just inside on a rough stone chair. In front of the priest stood a tall, stone pillar inscribed with the words "the face of the sun, the sacred hand, the morning star, and the new moon."

The priest then offered up songs and prayers as the sun rose over the Zunis' sacred peak, Corn Mountain. This daily ritual was performed over several mornings, and he then returned to the village to declare that spring had finally arrived.

In his notes, Cushing explains these actions. Each day the priest watched the sun as it rose further along the horizon, awaiting the time when the shadows cast by the sun on a natural monolith found on Corn Mountain and a tall stone pillar positioned by the

Astrologer-priest
This Toltec stone pillar, which dates back to the 8th century, is thought to show an astrologer-priest holding the staff that was used to fix a point for astronomical observation.

Solar signpost
The Inti Huatana, or hitching post of the sun, at Machupicchu, Peru.

Zunis fell into direct alignment. Thus, by regularly observing the shifting position of the sunrise, the sun-watching priest was able to confirm that the year had reached a turning point.

Tying the sun

The Inca peoples of South America are thought to have held ceremonies in which they employed shadows cast by the sun. At the mountain-peak citadel of Machupicchu, Peru, there is an unusual feature known as the Inti Huatana, "the hitching post of the sun." A rough granite megalith composed of an upright pillar on top of a natural pyramid-shaped spur projects from a platform containing a complex array of different planes, facets, recesses, and projections.

The name of the feature relates it to the Inca festival of Inti Raymi, performed each midwinter, during which the Incas "tied the sun" to prevent it swinging ever farther north in its daily progress.

It is unclear just how the Inti Huatana was used by the Inca peoples, or if any measuring devices were employed with it, but it is assumed that the upright pillar acted as what is known as a gnomon, a shadow-throwing device rather like the center of a sundial. The gnomon made it

58

♦ PAGE 60

SKYLINE CLOCKS AND CALENDARS

Many prehistoric peoples discovered that by noting the daily passage of the sun over various horizon features, they were able to measure the time of day and the orderly passage of the seasons. Some of these natural skyline clocks and calendars still work today.

THE TRADITION OF SUN-WATCHING was an important part of the culture of the Pueblo Indians of the American Southwest. In the 1930's, a study by anthropologist Alexander Stephen revealed that the Hopi Indians of Arizona used horizon calendars, in which the sun's position over specific features such as mountain peaks would tell the time of day and indicate the best time for important activities, such as planting, harvesting, hunting, and religious ceremonies.

From the roof of the ancestral house of the Bear Clan, the highest building in the Hopi village of Walpi, the peaks of Arizona's San Francisco mountains were visible 30 miles away. The Hopis used the southwestern skyline as a calendar to predict important events such as the winter solstice and the New Year.

The Soyal ceremony
The Hopi Indians also used this horizon calendar to predict the timing of the Soyal ceremony, which was the time when the *kachinas*, the ancestral spirits associated with the return of the rain, the growth of crops, and the continuity of life, were thought to return to the village from the mountain peaks. The Hopi sun priest would proclaim the arrival of these ancient spirits when he saw the sun setting in a specific notch on the mountains. This gave the Hopis 11 days to prepare for the celebration of the winter solstice.

One Hopi sun priest, Don Talayseva, explained in his autobiography, *Sun Chief* (1942), the necessity of keeping track of the seasons to indicate the important dates in the agricultural calendar: "When the sun arose at certain mountain peaks, it was time to plant certain seeds. On a certain date it was too late for any more planting. The old people said there were proper times for planting, harvesting, and hunting. In order to know these dates it was necessary for the sun priest to keep a close watch on the sun's movements."

California's Shasta Indians kept track of the calendar by watching the trees on the distant ridge. One of the trees would be struck by the first rays of the rising sun

---

The Hopi sun priest would proclaim the arrival of the ancestral spirits when he saw the sun setting in a notch on the mountain peaks.

---

on the solstices. The Shasta sunwatcher would also observe the trees on the western ridge that caught the last light of the sun as it set in the evening.

Horizon clocks and calendars were also part of the astronomy of the Old World. In Belgium and France, the positions of the sun relative to horizon features were known as *points de jours*, and there are several known horizon clocks in the Alps. At a position near the small village of Moos, at the northeast edge of the Dolomites, for example, the sun passes over three of the peaks in succession, at 11 A.M., noon, and 1 P.M., respectively.

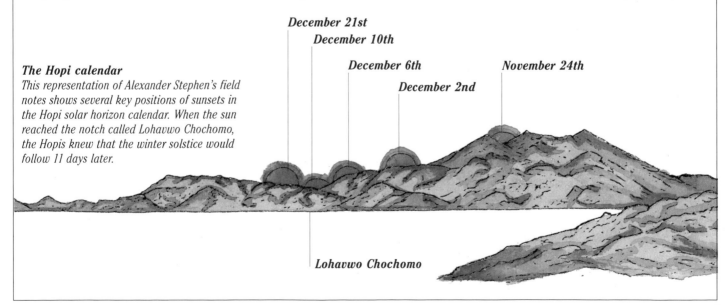

December 21st
December 10th
December 6th
December 2nd
November 24th

The Hopi calendar
This representation of Alexander Stephen's field notes shows several key positions of sunsets in the Hopi solar horizon calendar. When the sun reached the notch called Lohavwo Chochomo, the Hopis knew that the winter solstice would follow 11 days later.

Lohavwo Chochomo

easier to record the solstices, equinoxes, and displacements of the moon during its long cycle.

Shadow snake

In Mexico, shadows were used to produce more sensational effects. There is a stepped pyramid called the Castillo at Chichén Itzá, on the Yucatán Peninsula. The ancient pyramid was dedicated to Kukulcan, the Mayan version of the snake god Quetzalcoatl, the Feathered Serpent who brought the beneficent power of the sun god to all humans. In the last hour before sunset on the equinoxes, the stepped northwest corner of the pyramid throws a jagged shadow onto the balustrade of the northern staircase; the shadow resembles a serpent wriggling down from the top of the ancient pyramid. At the bottom of the balustrade is a stone serpent's head. When the shadow connects with the head, the illusion is complete.

Shadows and stones

Many prehistoric stones may have been designed with some kind of shadow play in mind. In 1976, British photographer

The Castillo shadow
On the equinoxes, the dying rays of the sun throw a "serpent shadow" down one side of the ancient pyramid at Chichén Itzá.

John Glover visited the ancient Castlerigg stone circle in Cumbria, England, to photograph the midsummer sunset over the stones. Just as the evening sun was sinking to the ridge, Glover happened to turn around and see the tallest stone of the circle, Latrigg, casting an immensely long, regular shadow across the valley. He later recalled the intense emotion he felt at that moment: "I felt projected into one of those fairytale situations when a secret path appears to show you the way to a beautiful hidden treasure."

Ancient sundial

Shadow formations are found at ancient burial mounds too. American artist and researcher Martin Brennan became convinced that the tomb at Newgrange and similar chambered burial mounds were actually complex forms of sun and moon dials that were designed to be used in conjunction with the shadows thrown by sticks of certain lengths.

At Knowth, Brennan discovered what appears to be a sundial on the flat top of one of the stones. Eight lines radiate in a semicircular fan from a central hole, which Brennan believes held a gnomon. If this engraving was indeed intended to be used as a sundial, then it is one of the oldest in the world, because the mound dates from around 3700 B.C. Brennan and other earth mysteries researchers believe that these phenomena provide evidence that ancient builders employed shadows and sunbeams for specific astronomical measurements that might have formed an integral part of their religious rituals.

Shadow paths
This photograph shows the shadow path at the winter solstice of one of the stones known as Long Meg and Her Daughters, in Cumbria, England.

THE HARVEST MOUND

The size and position of the ancient artificial mound, Silbury Hill in Wiltshire, England, allows a spectacular "double sunrise" to be seen at certain times of the year.

Silbury's huge shadow is thrown onto the gentle slope of a rise in the ground to the west of the hill. When this is viewed from the summit, a strange golden glow seems to emerge from the tip of the shadow and stretch almost to the western horizon.

Silbury Hill's impressive shadow "blessing the crops."

SILBURY HILL, the largest artificial mound in prehistoric Europe, stands 120 feet tall in the midst of the landscape around Avebury, in Wiltshire. One of prehistory's most enigmatic monuments, it was assumed to be a huge Bronze Age burial mound (*c.* 2000 B.C.) until 1969, when archeological excavation showed it to be much older, dating to around 2700 B.C. Furthermore, it contained no burial or inner chamber. What purpose could it have served?

Earth mysteries researcher Paul Devereux was able to show in 1989 that an intriguing phenomenon occurs at Silbury. If one looks eastwards from the flat summit of the hill, the contours of the far horizon and that of nearby Waden Hill nearly match one another. When the viewing position is lowered to a now partially eroded ledge about 17 feet below the flat summit, a short section of the distant skyline disappears behind Waden Hill. As a result of this double horizon, a striking "double sunrise" can be seen here at certain times of the year — once over the distant skyline from Silbury's summit and then minutes later over the top of Waden Hill, from a viewing position on the ledge.

Devereux found that this phenomenon occurred in early August, which was the important festival of Lughnasadh in the ancient Celtic calendar, and is Lammas (a celebration of the harvest festival) to Christians. A variety of archeologists have analyzed organic material taken from the heart of Silbury Hill, and some believe that the initial stages of its construction occurred in August. It seems plausible, therefore, that the spectacular double-sunrise phenomenon was engineered to celebrate the time of the harvest.

The "glory"

As the sunrise proceeds, Silbury's huge shadow is thrown onto the gentle slope of a rise in the ground to the west of the hill. When this is viewed from the hill's summit, a strange golden glow seems to emerge from the tip of the shadow and stretch almost to the western horizon. This remarkable optical effect is caused by the refraction of the light of the rising sun in dewdrops on the grass or cereal stalks in the fields. Such a phenomenon is known as the "glory." Impressionable observers have noted that Silbury Hill appears to be "blessing the crops." It seems likely that the mound's builders were aware of these striking effects. Thus Silbury Hill may be one more dramatic example of the use of lighting effects and shadow formations by ancient builders.

CHAPTER THREE

THE SACRED CENTER

From Delphi in ancient Greece to the Norse ash tree Yggdrasil to the Sun Pole of the Sioux Indians, every culture once had a sacred place that it believed to be the symbolic center of the world.

The supernatural was once believed to enter the world at its center, a sacred place often marked by what was known as a navel stone. It was through this stone that an imaginary vertical line or axis ran, and this axis linked the material world with the mystical, spiritual world.

Here, access might be gained to other worlds — heaven, hell, and the realms of spirits and the dead. The imaginary vertical line that runs through the center is often referred to as the cosmic axis because it places the earth at the center of the cosmos with heaven rising above it and the underworld yawning below. This sacred

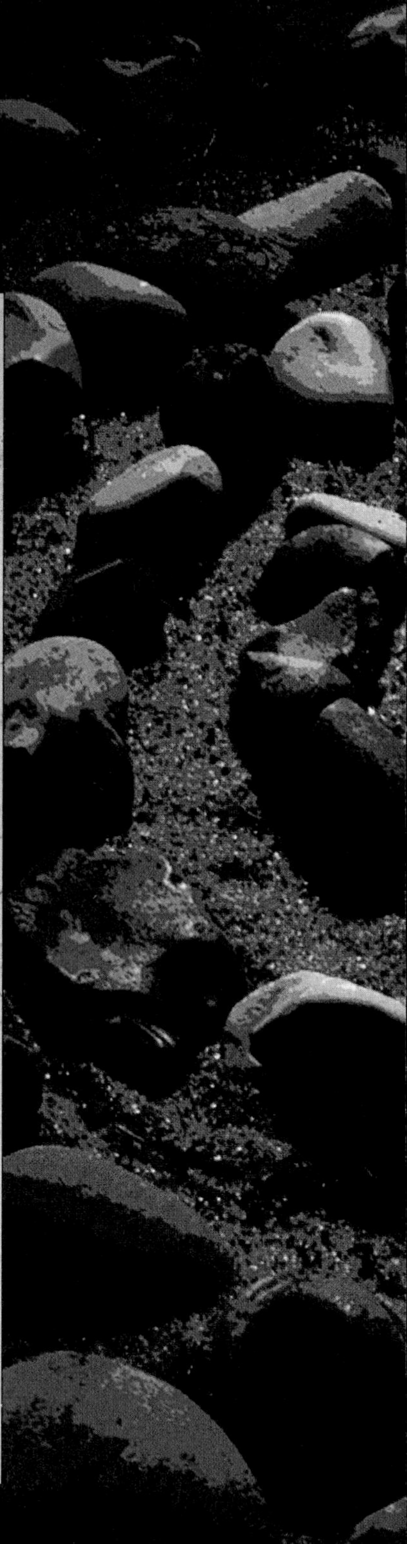

By locating and marking the center of the earth, ancient peoples hoped to chart the natural world and even gain control of it.

center is commonly known by its Greek name, *omphalos*, which means "navel." Thus the navel of the world, symbolically at least, is the point from which all life on earth springs.

Finding the center

To ancient peoples, locating the omphalos was essential to the creation of civilization, culture, and religion because it helped separate the safe, human world from the stormy, dangerous world full of natural forces. Because the sacred center of the world was believed to be so important, legends explaining how it was found occur in the mythology of almost every culture.

The people of ancient Greece, for example, believed that Delphi was the center of the earth. They thought the site was chosen not by human beings, but by the gods. According to myth, two eagles were sent out from the extremities of the earth by Zeus, the king of the gods; under the point at which their flight paths crossed, the

The omphalos stone
This stone marked the point that the ancient Greeks believed to be the center of the world. The swirling patterns may represent mysterious powers at the site.

sacred center of the earth, Delphi, would be found. To commemorate this myth, the artworks of ancient Greece often showed two eagles facing in opposite directions, perched on the sacred stone that marked the spot where their paths of flight intersected. Two such stones have been found at Delphi. One was a cone of gray stone shot through with quartz veins. Some scholars speculate that it was placed directly beneath the inner sanctum of the Temple of Apollo. A second elaborately carved stone is now in Delphi's museum. This sacred omphalos stone is rounded, about three feet high, and covered by a delicate interlaced pattern carved in bas-relief whose meaning is unknown. Some researchers claim that the pattern holds the key to mysterious powers that are active at the site. Other scholars believe, however, that they were just decorative, since such patterns are a common motif in primitive art. The Celtic peoples, too, carved a similar type of swirling design into stones found at Turoe in Ireland and Pfalzfeld in Germany.

Safeguarding the city

Medieval European cities often contained navel stones, which apparently helped ensure the continued luck and prosperity of the city. Among these are the London Stone; the stone at Tübingen, Germany, which every student at the university there had to touch for good fortune; and the "Blue Stane" found at St. Andrews, on the east coast of Scotland.

By locating and marking the center of the earth, ancient peoples hoped to chart the natural world and even gain control of it. From this, the best of all vantage points, the movements of the sun and

Umbilical cord to life
This beaded buckskin pouch in the shape of a lizard once contained the umbilical cord of a Plains Indian woman. This charm was believed to anchor the owner to this world, protecting her from harm and ensuring long life.

and west, might be fixed, and a calendar could be developed, of the ceremonial year, or of the different seasons, and of the best times for planting and harvesting crops.

moon might be observed against the distant horizon. Monuments, such as large standing stones or wooden poles, were frequently set up and used to chart the movements of heavenly bodies. Thus, using the sacred center, the cardinal directions, north, south, east,

Freeing the spirit
The guardians of the four directions look out from this Mimbres-Mogollon pottery bowl. It was broken more than 1,000 years ago at the death of its owner in order to free his or her soul.

Entering other worlds

The omphalos supposedly indicated the site of the cosmic axis leading from this world to other worlds. This axis was usually thought to run directly through the sacred center, and so formed a kind of umbilical cord to the spirit world.

The people who lived in Italy before the Romans, the Etruscans, believed that each city had to possess its own cosmic axis. Whenever they founded a new city, diviners were employed to locate the cosmic axis and suggest a suitable site for the omphalos. From this crucial focal point, they laid out four straight roads that were aligned to the four cardinal directions: north, south, east, and west. At the center the Etruscans hollowed out a shaft, which they called the *mundus*, or world. They filled it with offerings to the gods and goddesses and sealed it with a stone disc. The Etruscans believed that this shaft was the gateway to the

STANDING AT THE CENTER

The Dakota Indians fashion a special Sun Pole from a carefully chosen cottonwood tree for their Sun Dance. At the climax of the ceremony, they put offerings in a fork of the tree and sing:

At the center of the Earth,
Stand looking around you.
Recognizing the tribe,
Stand looking around you.

Focal point

The Dakotas were not the only people to believe that they stood at the center of the earth. Almost universally, all tribes, races, and peoples believed that they stood at the world's center. This belief, in a sense, is an extension of the human body's "directions" of front, back, and sides. Wherever we are, we are always "here," at the center of our world — the horizon seems to encircle us, while the sky appears to arch directly above our heads. Every person on earth sees himself or herself as being at the center of the universe. By the same token, a variety of sites all over the globe were seen by local peoples as the center of the world.

♦ PAGE 68

THE MAYPOLE

Today dancing around the Maypole is usually done by schoolchildren, but the Maypole once symbolized cosmic order, upholding the very laws of the universe.

MAY DAY ORIGINALLY MARKED the start of summer and the renewal of the earth's fertility. This rite has been observed in many cultures; the Romans, for example, made sacrifices to Maia, mother of Mercury, on the first day of her month. The May Day that is still celebrated in numerous parts of Europe, however, replaced a pagan ceremony, the festival of Beltine, which was held at the mid-point of the Celtic year to honor the sun and the mother-goddess.

Of the many May Day traditions, one of the most important is that of the Maypole. This relic of pagan tree worship originally represented the cosmic axis and the phallic power of the sky god. On May Day in medieval and Tudor England, villagers cut branches from woodland trees and carried them back to their houses. These boughs would then be used for decoration, to symbolize the process

Trade signs
In parts of central Europe, signs representing a town's main trades are fixed down the sides of its Maypole. Often made of painted metal, these images symbolize the authority of the local trade guilds. This example is from the Bavarian region of Germany.

The Maypole originally represented the cosmic axis and the phallic power of the skygod.

of rebirth. One focus of the annual ritual was the May Tree or Maypole, a young tree that was stripped bare except for its top boughs, which were left in place to indicate new life. Adorned with flowers and ribbons, the tree was brought back to the village, and erected there to serve as a focus for the May Day celebrations.

Festive dance
The English tradition of dancing around the Maypole with ribbons dates from the last part of the 19th century. Following the usual custom, each of these children is holding a ribbon, the other end of which is attached to the top of the pole.

Annual festival

In most parts of Britain, Maypoles were usually installed each year, and then taken down soon after May Day, but some were left in place permanently. Few of these remain, however, for in 1644, Oliver Cromwell's Puritan Parliament ordered them to be pulled down. Even after the British monarchy was restored, the Maypoles that had been destroyed by Cromwell were rarely replaced.

Similar rituals were also observed in Germany. Maypoles are often felled there on the evening before May Day, and put up on May Day morning. Permanent Maypoles frequently mark crossroads. In Bavaria, these are sometimes painted with a heraldic design in blue and white, the Bavarian national colors.

Evergreen ritual
The German town of Dudeldorf, in common with many others, has a conifer as its Maypole. Like the early English Maypoles, this is stripped of all its branches except for those at the top, which represent new life. Sometimes, a broomstick is attached to the top of the tree in place of the uncut foliage.

Dance of life
Dancing around the Maypole
confirms the interconnectedness
of all life: the pole is the center,
the ribbons symbolize chance.

> **This axis is a magical place. Here opposites come together. Time and space are wiped out; the four seasons merge and the opposing principles of yin and yang are in eternal harmony.**

underworld. Once a year, at the festival of Larentalia in December, the stone disc sealing the shaft was lifted so that the priests could make offerings of fruit and vegetables to the spirits of the dead who were believed to inhabit the underworld.

Cosmic axis

Around the world, many peoples speak of a mystical vertical axis running above and below the earth, linking it with other planes of existence, such as heaven and hell. This axis is a magical place. In an ancient Chinese book of rites, the *Chou-li*, it is described as the place where the earth and sky meet, the *Chien-mu*. Here opposites come together. Time and space are wiped out; the four seasons merge and the opposing principles of yin and yang are in eternal harmony.

The cosmic axis takes many different forms. The Welsh bards, for example, sang of four separate circles linked by the cosmic axis: *Annwn*, the underworld; *Abred*, the physical earth; *Gwynyyd*, the heavenly upperworld; and above them all, *Ceugant*, the realm of the creator.

Kenyab sundial
For the Kenyab people of Borneo, the cosmic axis is a carved pole set in the ground. The pole is also used as a sundial to determine when to plant their crops.

One of the simplest expressions of this linkage of heaven, earth, and omphalos is a custom of the Kenyab tribesmen of Borneo. For the Kenyab, the center is a carved, ritual pole of fixed length set in the ground. It throws a shadow that is carefully measured at noon on several successive days. When the shadow begins to shorten from its maximum length, the time for preparing the land has finally arrived. In some tribal societies, the length of the shadow cast by a ritual pole on a given day forms the radius for marking the boundary of a ceremonial building.

Stairway to heaven

The Mayas see the axis as a ladder with 13 rungs rising up from earth and leading to the heavens, and nine rungs going down to hell. Each step is occupied by a deity. Other cultures see the cosmic axis as

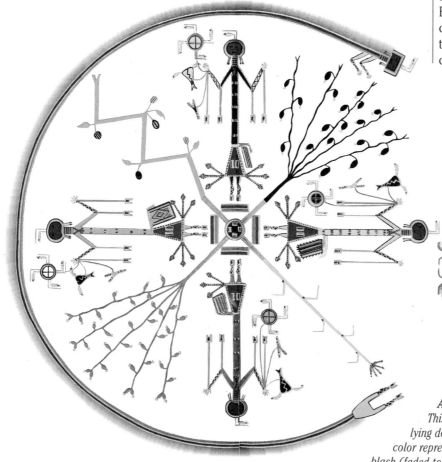

A divine compass
This Navajo sand painting depicts four gods lying down in the shape of a cross. Each body color represents a different cardinal point: north is black (faded to dark brown), at the top of the design.

◆ PAGE 70

As in Heaven, So on Earth

The Quechua Indians of Peru have oriented their village to reflect the movements of the Milky Way as it rotates above them, making an imaginary X across the night sky.

A MODERN USE OF THE SACRED center that connects the movements of the heavenly bodies with the pattern of life on earth is described by anthropologist Gary Urton of Colgate University, New York, in his book, *At the Crossroads of the Earth and the Sky* (1981). The book presents his research into the sky lore of the Quechua Indian village of Misminay, near Cuzco, Peru.

The Indians of this region are the direct descendants of the Incas. Like their ancestors, they see the Milky Way as the most important feature of the night sky and believe that the activities of the Milky Way rule earthly phenomena such as rain, water, and even fertility.

The heavenly cross

From any fixed point in the Southern Hemisphere the night sky appears to be in constant motion overhead. Above Misminay, the Milky Way appears to rotate so that its southern and northern ends rise alternately every 12 hours from the southeast and northeast, respectively. In a 24-hour period, this apparent rotation seems to make two lines across the sky that intersect directly overhead. *Cruz Calvario* ("Cross of Calvary") is the name of the point where they intersect.

This way of perceiving the night sky goes back at least to Inca times. It is reflected on the earth below in the layout of Misminay: two footpaths and irrigation canals running side by side form an X-shaped cross. Their intersection is called *Crucero* ("crossing") and its position is marked by a church. This corresponds to the crossing point of the Milky Way, *Calvario*, in the sky directly overhead.

The Quechuas recognize some constellations that are made up of chains of bright stars, but most of their constellations are seen as dark areas in the sky. They

appear like silhouettes against the brighter background of the Milky Way. These dark constellations are closely observed by the Quechuas in order to predict when it will rain, so that they will know when to plant their crops. As the start of the rainy season nears, the dark clouds in the Milky Way gradually become more and more indistinct as increased moisture in the air reduces the visibility of the skies.

The people of Misminay call the Milky Way *Mayu*, which means "river." For them it is a heavenly version of the Vilcanota River, which flows from southeast to northwest near their village.

Their myths say that the waters of the river flow over the edge of the earth into the encircling void of the heavens and are collected in the northwest by the Milky Way. The Milky Way then carries them underground before rising in the east. As the waters are carried overhead, some of the moisture falls to earth again as rain. The celestial and terrestrial rivers are thus linked in a mythical recycling of the waters, fertilizing land and sky.

An Andean world view
The church at the center of Misminay is beneath the point where the apparent rotation of the Milky Way seems to make a cross in the sky. The X-shape of the canals and paths reflects this cross. The Milky Way is thought to carry the waters of earthly rivers under the globe, and return them as rain. Orienting the map to the east accords with the worldview of the Quechua people.

Looking out from the center

Crucero is the spot in Misminay from which the village and the horizon beyond is divided into four quarters. The Quechuas, like the Incas before them, use the intercardinal directions: southwest, southeast, northeast, and northwest. Each direction has its own mythic significance, reflected in house groupings in the village and in the sacred peaks beyond. The northwest-northeast quarter, for example, is associated with the ancestors; the holy mountain visible on the distant horizon is called *Apu Wañumarka* ("Storehouse of the Dead").

In the creation myth of the Zuni Indians of western New Mexico, the first Zunis wandered for a long time, looking for the center, a place of peace and stability, where they could settle. But they could not find it. Frustrated, they finally called on their insect god K'yan asdebi, "Water-Skate," in the hope that his long legs could point to all six directions at once, thus identifying the sacred center.

This he did for them, by rising to the zenith and stretching out his legs to the six directions: the four cardinal points plus above and below. Gradually, he moved his body downward and said: "Where my heart and navel rest, beneath them mark the spot and there build a town of the midmost, for there shall be the midmost place of the earth-mother, the navel."

Zuni mask
On this mask the six directions (the cardinal points plus above and below) are represented by six different colors.

consisting of various levels of existence. But whatever form it takes, its purpose is to maintain as well as to symbolize order in the natural world.

The tree of life
The tree of life, also known as the world tree, is found in most cultures. It supports the universe and maintains the order of the cosmos. Its roots are often said to be in the underworld, its trunk to rise through this world, and its branches to be in the heavens. At the tip of the tree is a bright star: In the Northern Hemisphere this is often known as the North Star, which seems to be a still point in the midst of the whirling, chaotic skies.

Yggdrasil, the world tree of ancient Norse mythology, was revered because it contained every aspect of the world and represented continuity. Drawings of the great ash tree were commonly carved on runestones, hundreds of which can still be seen throughout Scandinavia.

The world tree, in particular, often marked the site of the omphalos. The Yakuts of Siberia believed that "at the golden navel of the Earth" stands a tree with eight branches. The symbolic use of trees to mark the center of the world can also be found in traditional cultures as varied as those of the Indians of America and the Australian Aborigines.

Sacred wood
Among the many Plains Indian tribes, visions were often sought in rituals that used the power of a sacred tree. Black Elk was an Oglala Sioux medicine man who encountered the world tree, which for the Sioux is a cottonwood, during a vision. In the vision he visited Harney Peak in the Black Hills of South Dakota. He was also given wooden objects (a bow, a cup, and a stick that turned into a sacred tree) by the spirits which he was told would enable him to fulfill the vision and heal his people.

For the ancient Germanic people, the cosmic axis existed in reality as well as in myth. A wooden pillar called *Irminsul* stood in the center

The Norse world tree
In this 19th-century illustration, the branches of the world tree form heaven, the earth is the middle, and the roots are in hell.

of a sacred enclosure at Obermarsberg until Emperor Charlemagne destroyed it in A.D. 772 as part of his effort to convert the pagan Germans to Christianity.

But the tradition of the cosmic axis did not entirely die out with the coming of Christianity to Europe. In some parts of Germany and Holland, it was the custom to train linden trees to grow in the shape of the axis. As the tree grew taller, it was trimmed so that it had three or four disc-like layers of foliage around the trunk. Frequently, the lowest level supported a wooden floor on which people were able to dance during festivals.

Mountain myths
In Persian mythology, the world tree is called *Gokart*. It grew from the ocean on the first day of creation and is vital to the well-being of the whole universe, for it was thought to prevent death by yielding the nectar of immortality.

Other peoples thought that the cosmic axis was a sacred hill or holy mountain. According to Persian legend, a mythical mountain called Haraberezaiti (Elburz) in Georgia is believed to be at the center of the world. Its peak touches the sky: the sun, moon, and stars revolve around it. Further east, in India, the Hindus revere Mount Meru. Like Haraberezaiti, it has many levels, with the North Star at its summit. The great stepped pyramids of Mexico, the temples of Cambodia, and the ancient ziggurats of Babylon are all man-made representations of mountains. Inside these sacred places the mysteries of the underworld were celebrated.

In the Book of Genesis, the serpent tempts Eve to eat the forbidden fruit of the tree. In myth and legend throughout the world, a serpent often snakes around the tree of life, threatening the stability of the cosmic axis. In Norse mythology the world serpent coils around Yggdrasil, the world tree. When he writhes, the earth shudders, but no matter how much the snake moves, the axis remains firm — a symbol of continuity and stability.

At the center of the maze

In Europe, grass labyrinths were laid out around a central upright, often a tree, stone, or cross. The turns of the labyrinth were believed to symbolize the world serpent, while the upright at the center of the maze perhaps stood for the cosmic axis. Some ancient maze names hint at the mythological role of the serpent: the ancient grass labyrinth at Steigra, south of Leipzig in Germany, is known as the *Schlangengang* ("snake path"). And the

---

In trances, shamans ride up the cosmic axis into the heavenly upper world or down into the underworld.

---

grass labyrinth in the Eilenriede Forest, Hannover, Germany, still contains a large linden tree growing at its center.

Another symbolic representation of the world tree is the Maypole. The spiral patterns often painted around it may represent the serpent ascending and descending the cosmic axis. The magical properties of the axis were believed to allow human beings access to the spirit world. Ancient peoples thought that the

spirits could speak at omphalos sites. At Delphi in ancient Greece, the oracle had her temple and foretold the future.

Shamanic journeys

From North America to Mongolia, shamans, the healers and visionaries of the ancient world, used spiritual techniques to gain access to other worlds, or other states of consciousness, through the cosmic axis. In the myths and legends of virtually every culture, the gods, goddesses, and heroic mortals also used the cosmic axis to journey between different worlds.

In their trances, shamans ride up the cosmic axis into the heavenly upper world or down into the underworld. In some cultures, the shaman literally climbs a tree or pole to reach heaven. Among the Koryak of Siberia, shamans climb a post in the middle of the ritual hut, into which steps have been cut, making the post a stairway to heaven.

A universal concept

Most ancient peoples possessed some concept of the symbolic center of the world. The sacred center could take the form of a special stone, as at Delphi, a holy city like the Inca Cuzco (the name means "navel" in the Quechua tongue), or, for the Semang people of the Malay Peninsula, a large rock where their god, Batu-Ribn, is believed to emerge at the center of the world.

Enter the spirit
In Haiti, voodoo shrines have a central post called a poteau-mitan *through which the* loa *("spirit") is believed to enter during ceremonies and possess the spirits of those dancing around the pole.*

The tree of life
This modern Mexican tree of life shows Adam and Eve at the top, the globe in the center, and the stages of human life from birth to death around the edges.

The Center of the Labyrinth

The twisting symbol of the labyrinth has been traced back over 3,500 years. It occurs in different cultures, at different points in time, in places as diverse as Peru, Arizona, Scandinavia, Germany, France, Italy, Crete, Egypt, and India.

THE DESIGN OF THE LABYRINTH symbol consists of a single meandering pathway that leads from the entrance to the center. Throughout the world and throughout history, it has been carved on wood and rock faces, woven into the design on blankets and baskets, laid out on the ground in the desert and on shorelines, in colored stone or tiles on the floors of villas, churches, and cathedrals, and cut into the living earth on village greens and hilltops. Occasionally the design of the labyrinth itself is altered or developed, but usually it is utilized with no significant variation.

The labyrinth has often been employed as a symbol for the omphalos, the sacred center, or the navel of the world. Some ancient Roman mosaic labyrinths were

> ## The labyrinth stood as a symbol of Christian faith, making it clear to the faithful that there is only one path to the center.

surrounded by a depiction of fortified walls; the center of the labyrinth represented the various cities of the Roman Empire. In medieval, Christianized Europe, the labyrinths appeared in churches and cathedrals. The centers of some of these were designated as Jerusalem, the Christian holy city. In this instance the labyrinth stood as a symbol of Christian faith, making it clear to the faithful that there is only one path to the center, just as there is only one true path to salvation.

Labyrinths of the Americas
In the Americas, the labyrinth is etched into the sands of the Nazca Plain in Peru, and scratched on boulders and rock faces in northern Mexico, New Mexico, and Arizona. Among the Hopi people of Arizona it is known as *Tápu'at* (Mother and Child), and is depicted in two forms. There is a circular variety symbolizing the Sun Father, the giver of life; the various lines and pathways represent the road of life that should be followed, and the four points where the lines end represent the four

A prehistoric maze
Thousands of surface engravings, including intricate maze patterns, decorate a vast area of rocks in Capo di Monte, northern Italy. The engravings date to around 2500 B.C.

Labyrinth of the Basilica of St. Quentin in France

CHRISTIAN LABYRINTHS
Pavement labyrinths, constructed in colored stone or tiles and usually between 10 and 40 feet in diameter, are often found in the great early medieval churches and cathedrals of Europe. The design is similar to that of the ancient labyrinth and is based on the equal-armed cross. In a few cases the Christian mazes still bore a representation of Theseus and the Minotaur at the center.

Fun and games
Some of these mazes were the scene of symbolic games and dances; a game known as *pelota* (similar to jai alai) was played at Easter on the pavement labyrinth in the cathedral at Auxerre.

These labyrinths were probably walked as a substitute for long pilgrimages. The labyrinth design symbolized the tortuous path that every good Christian followed in his or her pursuit of redemption, and the pattern of Christ's own preordained life and inevitable fate. They therefore acted as an aid to religious contemplation.

cardinal points. Within the square variety, the lines are subtly interconnected to produce one labyrinth within another: the Mother Earth symbol, depicting the unborn child within the womb of its mother and cradled in her arms after birth. The Hopi Indians also see the labyrinth as a symbolic representation of the concentric boundaries of their traditional lands, which have secret shrines hidden at several key points around their perimeters.

The Tohono O'otam and Pima tribes from southern Arizona weave baskets from dried leaves, stems, and roots of various desert plants. The labyrinth appears on these as a design known as "The House of Iitoi." It explains the myth of Iitoi, the ancestral founder of the tribes, whose spirit resides at the top of Baboquivari Peak, one of the sacred centers of the tribal lands.

From time to time Iitoi's spirit, in the form of a small man, would apparently sneak into the nearby villages and cause trouble. He would escape by confusing his pursuers with his circuitous route back up the mountain. The design shows Iitoi on the tortuous path to the sacred center of Baboquivari Peak.

European mazes
In Europe the labyrinth symbol is widespread and varied in its forms. Prehistoric labyrinth designs are found carved on rock faces at Pontevedra, Spain, and at Val Camonica in northern Italy. But the most famous ancient labyrinth was at Knossos in Crete, where the monstrous bull-man known as the Minotaur was supposed

to be imprisoned. The Labyrinth itself, a Minoan palace/temple complex, was destroyed and then rebuilt several times during its long history, but was eventually abandoned c.1380 B.C. No examples of the labyrinth symbol survive from the site itself. A variety of Cretan coins, however, incorporate a type of labyrinth design; these ancient coins date from the last three centuries before Christ.

The labyrinth symbol was widely used and adapted by the ancient Romans; its geometric form was a popular subject for depiction in mosaic pavements, of which there are more than 60 known examples. They are found throughout the Roman Empire and in North Africa.

Turf designs
Turf labyrinths, or turf mazes as they are popularly known, were once found in many countries throughout Europe. They are formed by ridges of turf and shallow trenches marking a single pathway that commonly leads to a small mound at the center. Most were between 30 and 60 feet in diameter and circular, although square and other polygonal examples are also known. Several hundred sites have been recorded, but only 11 examples survive — eight in England and three in Germany. Although such mazes have been known since early Roman times, most of those recorded probably date to medieval times. Folklore and the scant records that survive suggest that mazes were a popular feature of village spring fairs. Some turf mazes

Dead center
A maze at the center of a cross marks a grave in the north of England.

can still be found on village greens, or commons, often close to churches, but others are found on hilltops and at other remote sites, hinting at a link with earlier pagan traditions and customs.

The world tree
Three of these mazes have fully grown trees at their centers. These trees provide a link between the symbolism of the omphalos, or navel of the world, and the symbolism of the world tree, or tree of life. To the roving Vikings of Scandinavia, this was the world ash tree (Yggdrasil in the ancient Norse language), whose long branches reached up to heaven. The turf maze at Saffron Walden, England, has

---

Since spirits were believed to be able to travel only in straight lines, the turns of the maze kept them from escaping.

---

now lost its large ash tree, but otherwise survives in good condition. There is an 18th-century account of how young men would race each other through the maze to reach young women standing at the center. In both spiritual and secular use, the labyrinth design seems to symbolize the long and complex path that must be followed in order to reach the object of the quest at the center.

Dances and processions took place at the *Rad* ("wheel") turf maze in Hannover, Germany; a mature lime tree stands at the center, making it one of the most impressive surviving turf mazes. Slupsk in Poland formerly possessed an enormous turf maze, around 150 feet in diameter, which was used as the site for a costumed festival administered by the local shoemakers' trade guild.

A stone maze for luck at sea
In Scandinavia stones were often used to mark out the labyrinth design; over 500 examples have been recorded. Stone labyrinths also existed in Iceland, Russia, and the various Baltic countries, India, Arizona, and the British Isles. Many of the Scandinavian labyrinths are found close to the coast, and were built by fishing communities, probably during the medieval period, when labyrinths were occasionally painted on the walls of churches in the region. Until the early part of the 20th century, many Scandinavian fishermen would walk the labyrinths before putting out to sea to ensure good catches and favorable winds. It was believed that unwelcome winds might be trapped and neutralized in the circuitous coils of the labyrinth.

Trapping the souls of the dead
Some stone circles are found far inland, high in the hills near ancient grave sites, often dating from the Bronze Age. The stone labyrinth known as the Rösaring at Lassa, Uppland, Sweden, is situated at the end of an ancient road built c. A.D. 815, along which it is probable that the dead were pulled on carts to their burial. The souls of the dead ancestors may have been thought to reside here. Since spirits were believed to be able to travel only in straight lines, the turns of the maze kept them from escaping and causing trouble.

The labyrinths were also believed to protect the living from the perils of the supernatural world. The shepherds and hunters of Lapland would walk along the labyrinths to escape from trolls and other forms of evil spirits, who they believed would follow them in. Once inside the maze, however, the theory was that the underworld spirits would be trapped, unable to find their way out of its center.

Tibetan tangle
This endless knot from Jokhand Temple in Lhasa symbolizes the unity of all things.

Amazing speed
The people who live near this maze in the south of England claim that a man could run from the maze to a spot half a mile away and back in the time it would take another man to run around the maze.

JERUSALEM

Often seen as the center of the world, Jerusalem is the archetypal holy city, a sacred place for three religions: Judaism, Christianity, and Islam.

EARLY JEWISH TRADITION names Jerusalem as the center of the world. Later religious scholars taught that the world was like a man's eyeball: the white was the ocean surrounding the world, the iris was the world itself, and the pupil was Jerusalem. The image in the pupil was of a Jewish temple, built at the center of the world. The core of Jerusalem — its most sacred place and the reason for its existence — is Mount Moriah, a natural outcrop called the Rock.

New religions often reuse the sacred sites of older ones. At least six religions have worshiped on Mount Moriah. In pre-Jewish times, the Rock was a Canaanite "High Place," where the sky god Baal was worshiped in

> **Scholars taught that the world was like a man's eyeball: the white was the ocean surrounding the world, the iris was the world itself, and the pupil was Jerusalem.**

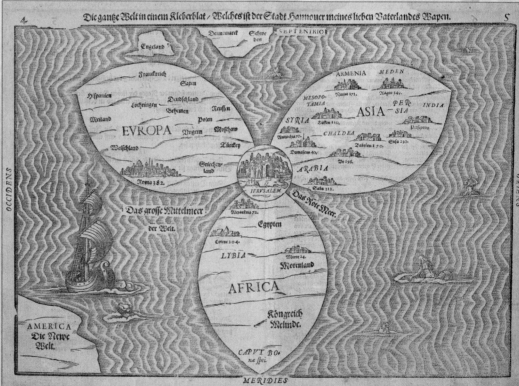

the open air. Abraham prepared to sacrifice Isaac there. After King David conquered Jerusalem about 1000 B.C., the Rock became the *kibleh*, or "point of adoration." Later, Solomon erected his temple there.

Subsequently, there was a second Jewish temple, then a Greek shrine dedicated to the most powerful of the Olympian gods, Zeus. The final Jewish temple, built by Herod the Great, was destroyed by the Romans in A.D. 70. Today, the Western, or Wailing, Wall is the only remaining part of Herod's temple.

The center of the world
This 16th-century German woodcut illustrates the role set out for Jerusalem in the Old Testament Book of Ezekiel 5:5, where God declares: "This is Jerusalem; I have set her in the center of the nations, with countries round about her."

When the Romans destroyed Jerusalem, they erected a temple of Jupiter on the Rock. After the Roman Empire became Christian, a church took the place of the Roman temple. Finally, when the Islamic armies conquered Palestine in A.D. 638, the church was replaced by a mosque, which still occupies the site today.

The Islamic tradition

Below the Rock is the "well of the souls," a cave with a passage leading upward. Symbolically, this links the underworld and the upperworld. Legend tells that Noah's flood disappeared down this passage, and the prophet Muhammad ascended to heaven through it.

The mosque, whose beautiful gilded dome encloses the bare rock surface, is called the Dome of the Rock (*Qubbat al Sakrah*). The building's form, a central cupola surrounded by an attractive octagonal ambulatory (a type of sheltered walkway), symbolizes the center of the world. After Mecca, the Dome of the Rock is the most sacred place in Islam.

Holy Sepulcher

Medieval Christians, who believed that the earth was flat, also thought of Jerusalem as its center. Ancient maps, such as the *Mappa Mundi* kept in Hereford, England, show a platelike world with Jerusalem at its center as the navel of the earth. In turn, at the center of Jerusalem was the *compas*, the center of the world.

The Church of the Holy Sepulcher was built over the center above the reputed tomb of Christ, next to the place where He was crucified. In turn, Christ's cross was said to have stood over the burial place of Adam. Like the Dome of the Rock, the Holy Sepulcher Church was centrally laid out; it is circular.

From the Holy Sepulcher, according to Christian belief, both heaven and hell could be reached. The apocryphal *Gospel of Nicodemus* tells the story of

Christ's descent into hell to rescue the souls of the righteous (Adam, Abraham, Noah, and Moses were among them). Christ is believed to have entered hell through the burial tomb at the center of the world — the Holy Sepulcher — continuing the ancient Jewish tradition of gaining access to the underworld at Jerusalem.

Apocalyptic visions

Over the centuries, the great sanctity of these sites to three religions, Judaism, Christianity, and Islam, and many sects within those religions, has created conflict. In 1009 the destruction of the Holy Sepulcher led directly to the first Crusade during which Christian armies tried to wrest control of the Holy Land from the Muslims. In many parts of the holy city today, violent arguments continue to rage about which religion or sect owns certain sacred places.

All three of the religions whose sacred sites are found in Jerusalem believe that the holy city will be at the center of the events that will take place at the end of the world. In the Judeo-Christian tradition, for example, it is believed that an angel will stand in the city and blow the final trumpet, heralding the arrival of the apocalypse; while according to the teachings of Islam, the holy Kaaba, believed to be the most sacred place on earth, will journey from Mecca to Jerusalem on the Day of Judgment.

Christian shrine
The Church of the Holy Sepulcher, which was reputedly built over Christ's tomb.

Sacred dome
The Dome of the Rock was built directly over the spot from which the prophet Muhammad was believed to have ascended into heaven. After Mecca, it is the most sacred site in Islam.

Wailing Wall
This wall is all that is left of Herod's temple. Jews still come here to decry the destruction of the temple in A.D. 70. People also pray for help with their problems, writing them down and tucking the paper into cracks in the wall.

THE BLUE STONES

In ancient times certain blue stones established the link between king and country and were also used to mark out points in the landscape, such as crossroads. These stones were also thought to have been an essential part of the process of crowning the king.

THE STONE OF DESTINY

Beneath the medieval coronation chair in Westminster Abbey, there sits a slab of ancient sandstone in a specialized compartment. This ancient slab is called the Stone of Scone, the Coronation Stone, or more widely, the Stone of Destiny. Legend has it that this is the stone on which Jacob slept when he had his visionary dream of a multitude of angels ascending a ladder to the heavens above.

History of the stone

History tells us, however, that the stone came from Ireland. It was the royal omphalos stone upon which many ancient Irish kings were once crowned.

The mystical power of this stone was believed to be so great that in the 10th century it was moved to Scone in Scotland, where it was used in the inauguration of 34 Scottish kings. In 1296 the stone was brought to England by order of Edward I. By removing the stone from Scotland, he hoped to break the power of the Scottish kings.

IN ANCIENT TIMES, the union of the king, the ruler of the land, with his kingdom was often symbolized by a physical connection between the king and a stone. In some parts of Europe, certain special stones are also found in mosaics or set into walls and roads in ancient towns, marking out the very center of the city. Almost everywhere in Europe, stones have long been associated with kingship. The shaped stones were the most primitive representations of the earth goddess, and therefore the land.

The Dutch stones

Throughout the Netherlands blue stones mark the center of many cities. In the center of Schoonhoven, a deep blue stone is embedded in a 13th-century stone bridge over one of the canals. The bridge and the canal beneath it lie on the east-west, north-south axis. The stone is the focus of a mosaic that acts as a landmark indicating the center of the town. The mosaic is made from cobblestones forming two concentric circles, each of which is subdivided by 16 spokes radiating from the central blue stone and laid out to a traditional unit of measure called the *rijnlandse roed* (rod).

At another site, Nijmegen, a rectangular stone, replacing the original blue stone, marks the principal crossroads of the city. Up until the 20th century, funeral processions were conducted around this central spot.

The sacred Leiden stones

Each of the three blue stones found in Leiden is hexagonal and three feet in diameter. The oldest of these stones is set into the ground at the intersection of two roads. One of the roads is an ancient route that leads to a pre-Christian mound in the town associated with the Celtic god of light, Lugh, from whose name Leiden was derived. This ancient blue stone is set in the center of a circle of gray

The coronation chair
The Stone of Destiny, set beneath the coronation chair in Westminster Abbey, is still considered essential to the confirmation of the British monarch as ruler.

The union of
the king with
his kingdom was
often symbolized
by a physical
connection
between the king
and a stone.

The Schoonhoven Stone
This stone, at Schoonhoven, southern Holland, is a classic example of an ancient blue stone. Deep blue in color, the stone lies in the center of a decorative mosaic that marks the center of the city.

stone in medieval society, and suggests that its roots lie in Europe's pagan past.

Palmer found that this type of stone, which has been used since the Middle Ages, was imported from the Ardennes region of France. The region is thought to be named after Arduinna, a pagan goddess who was once worshiped there, suggesting that the stones are a survival of pagan beliefs into the Middle Ages.

An Ardennes blue stone, known as the Witches' Stone, survives to this day in the marketplace of Lier, in northern Belgium. The site was originally marked by a sacred oak under whose branches open-air courts were once held. The stone has the same dimensions as the blue stone at Schoonhoven and is also surrounded by the remains of a spiral mosaic.

stones and marks the precise spot where the four quarters of the medieval town met, as was the case at Nijmegen.

Like many other sacred stones, the blue stones at Leiden held a particular fascination for the local people. Dutch folklore tells that the Leiden blue stones were considered magical and sacred as late as the 17th century.

Pagan origins

Although there are many ancient blue stones in numerous cities throughout Europe, their full significance is still not known. A British artist and blue stone enthusiast, John Palmer, who has been researching the Dutch blue stones for many years, believes he has discovered the role of the blue

The pattern in the stones

Although only Schoonhoven now has a complete mosaic around its blue stone, Palmer has identified several more stones that were once set into mosaics. The blue stone in the main square of Amsterdam, for instance, was once surrounded by a vast circular pattern of stones.

The stones and the circular mosaics that once surrounded them may be a stylized echo of prehistoric stone circles, since these circles often have central stones as well.

Blue stones may have been associated with judicial activities that took place during the Middle Ages or even earlier. The stones reportedly marked the positions of open-air courts or assemblies in the medieval period. Some blue stones were used at sites where oaths were sworn. They also formed "seats" where traveling judges sat to pass laws and dispense justice when they came to an area.

The London Stone
Some stones were believed to confer authority on those who touched them. When the English rebel Jack Cade struck the London Stone with his sword and announced himself the Lord of London in 1450, he was symbolically taking possession of the city. A small remnant of this ancient stone can still be seen in London, in a niche in the wall of the Bank of China on Cannon Street.

◗ PAGE 82

MECCA

The Holy City of Mecca is the spiritual and physical center of Islam: every mosque in the world is oriented toward it, and five times a day Muslims face it to pray. Mecca was the birthplace of the founder of Islam, Muhammad, who lived from A.D. 570 to A.D. 632.

A T THE HEART OF MECCA, near the center of the court of the Great Mosque, is a small granite and marble shrine called the *Kaaba*, which Muslims consider the most sacred place on earth. The word Kaaba literally means "cube," a shape that represents the three dimensions of space: height, width, and depth. According to the teachings of the Koran, the Kaaba was first constructed by Abraham and his son Ishmael around a large reddish-brown rock called the Black Stone. This was given to them by the archangel Gabriel to become the cornerstone of a temple. Possibly meteoric in origin, the Black Stone is now encased in a large silver band and embedded in the exterior wall of the Kaaba at its eastern corner. Although Mecca itself has been rebuilt many times, the Black Stone has always remained intact in the wall of the shrine.

The right hand of God

For Muslims, the Black Stone is "the right hand of God on earth." It is kissed or touched by pilgrims at the beginning of the *tawaf*, the ritual of walking around the Kaaba seven times as Muhammad is thought to have done in A.D. 630 when he rededicated the site to Allah. It was Muhammad, too, who formalized the tradition of the *hajj* (pilgrimage) to Mecca, which all Muslims must make once in their lifetime. But he did not originate this idea; Mecca had been a place of pilgrimage since Abraham's day.

The marble shrine itself is rectangular, measuring about 39 feet long, 33 feet wide, and 49 feet deep. Because it is

intended to house the divine presence, its only furnishings are the three tall pillars that support the roof, and several hanging lamps made out of gold and silver. The present building dates from the 17th century, but the Saudi government made repairs to its walls and roof during the 1950's. For much of the year, the walls of the Kaaba are covered with a vast black and gold cloth called the *kiswa*, (meaning "robe"). This cloth is taken down every year, and replaced with a new one embroidered in the city of Mecca.

According to one Muslim sect, the Sufis, the Kaaba is the home of the soul, just as the heart may be thought of as the home of the soul within the body. The pilgrims themselves symbolize the blood of the world flowing around its spiritual heart. This heart is Mecca.

> **According to the Koran, the Kaaba was first constructed by Abraham and his son Ishmael around a large reddish-brown rock called the Black Stone.**

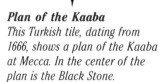

Plan of the Kaaba
This Turkish tile, dating from 1666, shows a plan of the Kaaba at Mecca. In the center of the plan is the Black Stone.

***The* kiswa**
*For most of the year, the walls of the Kaaba are surrounded by a huge cloth (*kiswa*) that is embroidered with verses from the Koran in 24-carat gold.*

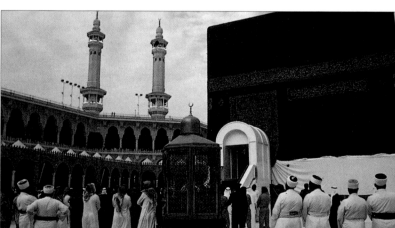

Palmer also claims to have discovered evidence of numerological symbolism in certain blue stones and the mosaics that often surround them. He suggests that the number of stones contained in these decorative arrangements may relate to the procedures or numbers of leading officials present at gatherings of judges and lawmakers.

King stones

Celtic kings were once inaugurated standing or sitting upon sacred stones used only for this ceremonial purpose. Known as king stones, these stones may have symbolized the sacred marriage of the king to the earth goddess. For example, at Tullahoe, Ireland, which was the capital of Tyrone in medieval times, a stone throne was formed by placing three slabs against a boulder. The throne was used as the seat of many of Ireland's kings in the Middle Ages, but was finally destroyed by the English in 1602.

The most famous coronation stone in ancient Ireland, upon which the kings of that country were inaugurated, was the *Lia Fail*, which means "Stone of Destiny," on the hill of Tara. In a clear expression of the magical power of the king stone, the *Lia Fail*, so legend claimed, cried out at the moment the true king of Ireland was crowned.

In most of the ancient inauguration ceremonies that used a stone, the king-to-be either sat upon the stone or made close contact with it with his bare hands or feet. According to ancient beliefs, this contact enabled the earth currents to flow through the king's body, "charging" him with the special energies and vitality needed to exercise his unique powers as a representative of the gods upon earth.

The sacred center

The sacred blue stones appear to have had several functions: they indicated the position of geomantic centers (the mid-point or conceptual point of origin of a particular place), they were used in legal and royal ceremonies throughout the Middle Ages, and they may have served as objects of pagan worship. In addition, they represent a medieval expression of the ancient idea of the sacred center, a fixed point in the world around which everything revolved.

St. Columb's Stone
The marriage between the king and the earth was often symbolized by the monarch standing barefoot on a stone on which footprints had been carved, such as St. Columb's Stone in Londonderry, Northern Ireland.

THE LEGEND OF KING ARTHUR
The idea of the king stone is also alluded to in the story of King Arthur. For centuries past, his story has fascinated writers and historians. As a result, considerable myth and legend now surround this Celtic king – Arthur has even been described as "the sovereign of the western medieval world."

Arthur, legend recounts, was the son of Ygerene, the duchess of Cornwall, and Uther Pendragon, king of the British. Arthur succeeded to the throne at the age of 15, but he first had to prove his right to the kingship. He did this by drawing the magical sword Excalibur from a sacred stone in which it was embedded. The stone stood in the courtyard of a chapel in London. On the stone were apparently inscribed the words: "Whoso pulleth this sword from this stone is rightfully born King of all England." Although many sought to extract the magical sword, only Arthur succeeded.

The true king
The medieval illustration above shows the young Arthur miraculously withdrawing the sword Excalibur from a stone, confirming him as the rightful king of England.

THE MAGICAL STONE OF TARA

Tara, seat of the ancient kings of Ireland, was the legendary sacred center of the country. A magical stone, the Lia Fail, *stood there, and was said to emit a scream when the true king was crowned.*

TARA, A SACRED SITE SINCE the Neolithic period, when a passage grave now known as the Mound of the Hostages was built there *c.* 2100 B.C., is best known for its connections with the kings of ancient Ireland. At Tara, 20 miles northwest of Dublin, a huge oval enclosure called the *Rath na Riogh* ("Fortress of the Kings") stands atop the low mound. Archeologists believe that all earthworks at the site were used at one time as centers for public ceremonies. One earthwork is known as *Forradh,* which is Gaelic for "seat of kings."

The king of Ireland was chosen not by heredity but by druids who took part in mystical rituals in order to be able to recognize him. Five druids would assemble to find the king through a sacred vision. They would sacrifice a bull, but only one of them would eat its flesh. That druid was then wrapped in the bull hide and watched over by the other druids, who chanted the "spell of truth" over him. In a vision induced by this ritual, the chosen druid would see the future king of Tara. The man chosen to be king was then sent for and brought to the royal seat.

The sacred stone

The ability and even the physical appearance of the king were believed to be essential to the prosperity of the country. The king had to be perfect — any bodily defect would make him unfit to rule.

Before his inauguration the future king had to undergo a series of ordeals to test his stamina and fitness. After the kingship had been awarded to him, a series of prohibitions (*geissi*) were put upon him which regulated his conduct. Violation of these would lead to his own destruction and bring ill-fortune to his people. The king was inaugurated on or beside a stone shaped like a phallus and known as the *Lia Fail.* In Irish mythology, the *Lia Fail*

> The *Lia Fail* is one of the four talismans brought to Ireland by the *Tuatha Dé Danann,* the legendary godlike people of Danu. They brought the stone from the northern islands of the world where they had learned druidism and magic.

is one of the four talismans brought back to Ireland by the *Tuatha Dé Danann,* the legendary godlike people of the goddess Danu. They brought the stone from the northern islands of the world where they had learned druidism and magic. The stone is believed by scholars to have symbolized the king's own fertility and the fecundity of the land under his rule. According to legend, "It used to cry out beneath every king that would take Ireland." The stone still stands beside the Mound of the Hostages.

The sacred marriage

After his inauguration, the newly appointed king was required to symbolically marry the goddess of the Sovereignty of Ireland. This ceremony (called the *Feis Teamhra*) bound the king forever to the land and its well-being. Little is known about the actual ritual involved, but scholars speculate that Ireland was represented in the ceremony by a white mare, since two of the sovereignty goddesses, Étain and Medb, were horse-goddesses in origin.

Researchers also believe, based on the account of Giraldus Cambrensis who wrote a history of Ireland in the 12th century, that the king was required to consummate his marriage to the mare, which was then killed and eaten by everyone present at the ceremony including the king himself. This rite was believed to confer upon him the kingship and dominion of the country, elevating the new king to the status of a god, since he had first married and then consumed the earth goddess.

The last ceremonial gathering at Tara, the legendary center of ancient Ireland, was held in A.D. 559 under the auspices of Diarmait, son of Fergus Cerrbel, king of Ireland. The sacred monarchy of Tara, steeped in pagan associations, probably came to an end with the coming of Christianity in the fifth century.

The Lia Fail, *or Stone of Destiny*

THE MAGIC JOURNEY

On the journey to the world of the spirits, the shaman sometimes climbed a pole, ladder, or tree that represented the cosmic axis. Or he banged a drum made of the wood of the world tree to show that he had begun his quest.

THE SHAMAN WAS THE ONE PERSON within the tribe who had the skill and power to undertake quests to the world of the spirits in search of special knowledge about the future or healing for the sick. Often the shaman ascended into the spirit world by physically climbing a tree or ladder that represented the world tree or cosmic axis.

Climbing the world tree

Many cultures believe that the world tree made the shamanic journey to other worlds possible. The tree stood at the center of three worlds, the upper world, the physical earth, and the underworld, and allowed the initiated to pass between these worlds. Climbing this world tree, or a pole that represented it, symbolized the inner journey of the shaman's soul.

In some cultures, in order to reach the otherworlds of spirit, the entranced shaman would embark on a visionary "journey" to the world tree, and would then climb it either to enter heaven or go down into the underworld.

In Siberian tradition the shell of the shaman's drum was made from a branch of this world tree. According to Romanian anthropologist Mircea Eliade, because of this connection with the world tree, the shaman, by his drumming, is "magically projected into the vicinity of the Tree."

In other traditions, the shaman climbs a tree, a notched pole, or a ladder to show that he is journeying to the spirit world. The Pomos of northern California, for example, climbed a pole 20 to 30 feet high during a four-day-long initiation ceremony. One day was devoted entirely to climbing the pole. In southern Africa figures teetering on top of ladders are frequently depicted in the shamanic rock art of the San people (once known as the Bushmen).

> **In Siberian tradition the shell of the shaman's drum was made from a branch of the world tree.**

Keeping spirit time
The Assiniboine Indians of the Great Plains practiced long periods of fasting to induce visions. This drum is decorated with spirit images that were probably inspired by the hallucinations fasting produced.

Trance dancer
Drumming and dancing were used by the shamans of the Kamchatka region of Siberia to induce trance states that would enable them to travel to the realm of the spirits.

Guidance from beyond
Spirit flight could be dangerous to the shaman, and in some traditions guides were used to help them on their journey. This "spirit guide," or "spirit helper," belonged to a 19th-century Mongolian shaman.

Powerful creature
Made by one of the Kama River tribes of Russia, this bronze image of a wild beast was believed by their shamans to have miraculous properties.

Stone-age shamans
This Paleolithic cave painting at Lascaux in France was painted c. 28,000–22,000 B.C. It depicts a ceremonial bird-stick lying next to a figure in a bird mask who was probably a shaman.

Shaman's rattle
American Indian shamans also use bird imagery to symbolize the shaman's flight. This Tlingit rattle is in the form of a bird, with a human figure and a frog sitting on top.

Hole-in-the-sky pole
Carved by the Tsimshian Indians of the Pacific Northwest, this wooden pole originally marked the ceremonial entrance to the house of Haidzemerks, one of their chiefs.

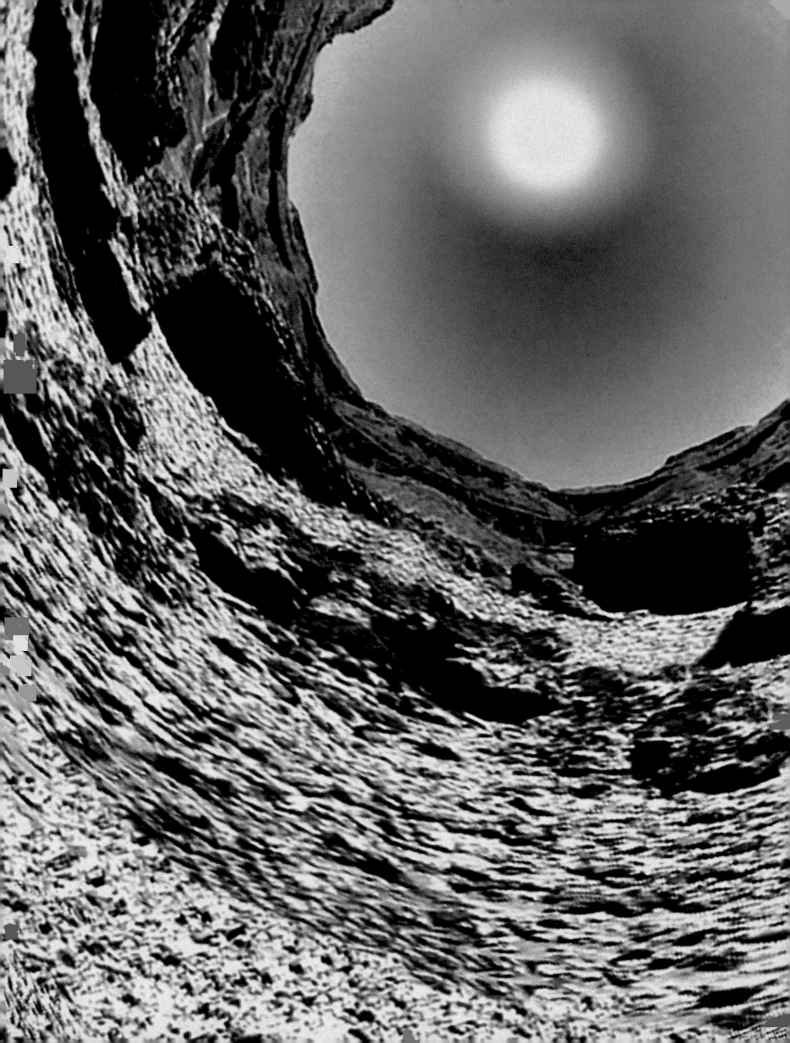

CHAPTER FOUR

MYSTICAL LANDSCAPES

Ancient peoples such as the Incas, the Celts, and the Greeks once believed that the landscape was the physical embodiment of spirits or gods. To the Incas, it also symbolized the social order and held the key to the calendar.

Ancient peoples believed the earth to be alive and the landscape and the heavens to exist in the form of deities. Within this living environment, they worshiped the earth and sky as gods and goddesses, often believing their kings and queens to be descended from them. To express their sense of unity with this natural, God-filled world, people constructed roads, drew lines and patterns across the land, and created vast earthworks.

Much of what these people left behind, in the lost cities of the Incas, in the sacred landscapes of Europe and Australia, and in the effigy mounds of the Americas, remains

The Inca empire
Cuzco was the capital of the Inca empire, which at its height around A.D. 1500 extended over a large area of South America. The Incas called the city Tawantinsuyu, *meaning "Four Quarters."*

A network of sacred lines
The 41 Inca ceques, or alignments, radiated from the Temple of the Sun out into the landscape around Cuzco. Sacred places lay along the ceques. This map is based on Inca scholar Dr. Tom Zuidema's initial research in Cuzco.

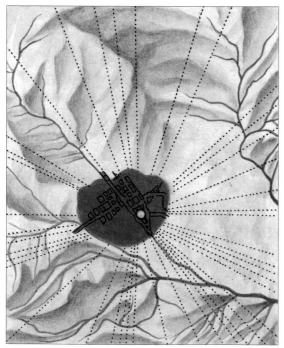

inexplicable. Yet some archeologists and anthropologists are beginning to unlock the intriguing secrets of some of these mystical ancient landscapes.

The Incas

More than 500 years ago, the Incas made changes to enormous areas of the South American landscape to make it more sacred. Around A.D. 1200 they began to amass an empire that stretched from present-day Ecuador in the north to Chile in the south. By building a variety of roads, cities, and shrines, the Incas created a symbolic landscape, one that combined ancestor worship, water symbolism, astronomy, ceremonial and and social activities. The capital and seat of the emperor, Cuzco, lay at the heart of this sacred Andean landscape.

The Incas believed that their emperor, himself called the Inca, was the son of the sun. And each year as the winter solstice neared (in June at the latitude of Cuzco), the emperor sat in a niche facing the sun in the Coricancha, or "Temple of the Sun" as the sun rose. Sheathed with gold and set with gems, the niche glittered in the sun's rays, thus "proving" the emperor's divinity to the people.

Divine intervention

For the Incas, Cuzco was the center of their empire. The Temple of the Sun stood in the middle of the city, its site chosen by a god.

God of gold
A mask representing the sun god, relic of an ancient Inca civilization.

Inca mythology tells that Manco Capac, the first Inca, who was sent to earth to spread civilization, used divine means to locate the site of the temple. He stuck a golden rod into the soil to find the right site: at the correct spot, the myths said, the golden rod disappeared into the earth. Manco Capac's golden rod may be a mythical reference to the cosmic axis, an imaginary vertical line that was believed by many different peoples to link the zenith with the mystical navel of the world or sacred center. This cosmic axis was believed to provide access to heaven, hell, and the spirit world.

Mysterious ceques

When the Spanish invaders arrived in Cuzco in 1533, they sacked the city and conquered its people. Their chroniclers, however, recorded some of what had gone before and been ruined. According

> ***Ceques* radiated out from the Temple of the Sun like rays from the sun.**

to their accounts, 41 *ceques*, which they translated as "lines," radiated out from the Temple of the Sun like rays from the sun, or spokes from the hub of a wheel. Yet they did not explain what the ceques, which no longer exist, looked like.

Many researchers now believe that the Spanish did not describe the ceques because they were never visible on the ground. They were probably not roads or even lines, but directions or alignments of Inca sacred places (called *huacas* in Quechua, the Inca language). These huacas could take many forms: standing stones or natural boulders, waterfalls or springs, temples, holy mountains, or caves. Modern scholars have located some of these sacred places. One of them is Tambo Machay, a ruined huaca outside Cuzco that also served as a lodge for the Inca. The temple of Pukamarka in the city itself is another shrine. There were apparently between 3 and 15 sacred places along any one ceque.

Counting the days

Yet scholars do not know what purpose the ceques actually served. It seems most likely that they had a number of different functions. One theory claims that they formed a huge calendar. The Spanish identified 328 huacas on the ceques around Cuzco; the Indians told them that each one represented a day of the year.

Dr. Tom Zuidema of the University of Illinois believes that the Inca year was in fact 328 days long and that this period related to a sidereal lunar calculation, which is founded on a $27\frac{1}{3}$-day cycle of the moon. Twelve of these sidereal lunar cycles added up to a 328-day period. The Incas did not count the 37 days that came at the end of

Inca messenger
This 17th-century drawing shows a knotted cord, called a quipu, which was used to encode information and was carried by runners who took messages throughout the far-flung Inca empire.

the year after the harvest, which, added to 328 days, make up our modern year of 365 days, the time it takes the earth to complete one full orbit of the sun.

The geography of the city itself was also sacred. Around 1440 the emperor Pachacuti divided Cuzco into quadrants. He laid out the principal buildings of the capital according to a regular pattern, which contained a strict social ordering. Thus the people of Cuzco lived in certain regions, based on the kinship groups (*ayllus*) to which they belonged. These in turn were related to the part of the empire from which their ancestors came.

Quartering the world

The city of Cuzco and the Inca empire beyond were divided into quarters. The *suyus*, or four quarters of the city, were believed to extend out to the farthest corners of the empire. The Huatanay River divided the city and the surrounding valley into two halves, one for the privileged, the other for the commoners.

The Inca road system had its hub in Cuzco at the great plaza of Haucaypata. There, four main roads met to form the dividing lines between the suyus. But the quarters of the city did not form a regular X-pattern: some were larger than others.

The main reason for this variation in size, according to modern

The southeastern quarter
The southeastern part of the empire and of the city of Cuzco were both named Collasuyu. *When in Cuzco, the Incas lived in the quarter of the city that related to the part of the empire from which they came.*

A shrine on a ceque
This spring is part of the ruined Inca shrine of Tambo Machay near Cuzco. Experts believe it is located on a ceque. The Incas thought that water, in the form of springs and rivers, was sacred. Ceques were often aligned along sources of water.

THE THIRSTY EARTH

To ensure that the earth would continue to absorb the waters of the flood, the Incas poured a variety of offerings into a hole in the ground in the central plaza of Cuzco, which they called Haucaypata but which is today known as the Plaza de Armas. This hole was known locally as the *ushnu* – literally, a person who can drink a great deal of beer without getting drunk.

The *mundus*

The Incas believed that the earth was thirsty because the sun dried the ground out. The ability of the earth to absorb water was vital, for there were floods during the rainy season each year.

The ushnu is very similar to the Etruscan landscape feature known as the *mundus*. These were large, ritually significant holes that the Etruscans dug in the centers of their cities in what is now Italy. They believed that the mundus itself marked the entrance to the sacred underworld.

experts, is that the suyu boundaries track the flow of water in the Cuzco valley, for instance in the form of rivers or canals. The boundaries assigned the right to use water to various kinship groups.

Towers to the sun

The Spanish chroniclers described how towers could be seen on the skyline near Cuzco. These high towers were used to indicate solar positions marking the key ceremonies of the year and the times for planting various crops, either at Cuzco or higher up the sides of the mountain.

Even though the Spanish destroyed the towers, Dr. Zuidema and Dr. Anthony F. Aveni of Colgate University were able to identify their positions, and found that there were four of them. Their work has also clarified the arrangement of the various ceques in and around the city. Although this system of towers was all on one ceque, the sun

Sun spot
From the Plaza de Armas in the center of Cuzco the Incas observed the movements of the sun.

was not seen along that ceque but from a point in the center of the Plaza de Haucaypata known locally as the *ushnu*. Historical reports and contemporary research both agree that only one solar sightline coincides with a ceque. In fact, probably only about a quarter of the 41 ceques held any astronomical significance. The Spanish claimed they had other functions, one of which may have been connected with the flow of water.

Spirit connection

The huacas on the ceques were often located where the flow of water changed direction, such as at the bend of a river or where two rivers met. The spirit world was also related to water. According to Aveni, the kinship groups received "water directly from their ancestors who were believed to reside within the earth." The ceques, some of which were located near rivers, were thus sacred to the ancestors of the kinship groups that lived in the area.

The Incas are also thought by modern scholars to have believed that water was brought by the Milky Way. Evidence for

> The ceques, some of which were near rivers, were sacred to the ancestors of the kinship groups that lived in the area.

this comes from the modern descendants of the Incas, the Quechua Indians. They still call the Milky Way *Mayu*, or "river" and believe that it is a celestial river that each night carries the water back from an ocean that lies beneath the earth to the sources of the rivers in this world.

Working from Spanish descriptions of the system, Zuidema and Aveni tried to trace the outline of the ceques in the landscape. They found that all of the ceques run in straight lines and believe that they were special sight lines, taken by looking from a fixed point toward the horizon. They passed over the hilly land around the city of Cuzco, often seeming to go beyond the horizon.

The kinship groups were responsible for worshiping at the holy places along their ceques at certain times of the year. The ritual year rotated through the land around Cuzco, as the huacas on the ceques became ceremonially active. At such times the huacas may have been tended by the kinship group that lived nearby, visited by pilgrims, or used as staging posts on the journeys of the children who were on their way to be sacrificed. Some adult human and animal sacrifices may also have been carried out at the huacas.

Resting on Inca walls
The church of Santo Domingo is built on the site of the Temple of the Sun. Its niches are not typically Spanish: they echo the niches in which the Inca once sat to greet the sun.

The ceques also helped to order the territorial relationships between groups. They may also have determined how they organized cooperative ritual and work activities, and even intermarriage. "In sum," says Aveni, "the ceque system may be considered a rather complex kinship map based upon residence and ancestor worship."

Pathways for pilgrims

The ceques may also have been used as pilgrimage routes. Zuidema has traced one such route that began at one of the shrines in the ceque system, Huanacauri, a sacred mountain. The pilgrimage route extended far beyond the valley.

The pilgrimage took place in June and was undertaken to celebrate the birth of the sun. The arduous route followed a straight line through the mountains to a place at the head of the Vilcanota River where the Incas believed the sun had been born, a place called La Raya by the Spanish. La Raya is a remarkable natural site: hot springs steam at the foot of a glacier, and since it is on the continental divide, the rivers that begin there run in two directions. The journey back, which was no longer sacred and therefore no longer needed to follow the landscape line, was easier, for the pilgrims walked along the river. Zuidema suspects that the pilgrimage route may even have extended beyond La Raya to the Island of the Sun in Lake Titicaca, some 200 miles away. But although several of the ceques were used for ritual walking, it is likely that they served more often as specific alignments of huacas or places of worship.

The Inca ceques appear to have been a type of ancient, straight track, much like leys, the alignments discovered in the 1920's in Britain by Alfred Watkins. Watkins thought that the lines he had discovered crisscrossed Britain and were traces of ancient tracks.

But while evidence about the form and function of leys has been lost, research in Cuzco has uncovered information about the ceques that sheds light on their role in Inca life.

The Inca ceques seem to have been used both as a symbol of the divine and as the framework of the social order. It is impossible to say conclusively that lines on the landscape in other cultures might have had the same meaning, but a better understanding of the Inca ceques may provide an insight into the way such lines could have been used.

Toasting the sun
The painting on this wooden cup shows two Incas carrying cups. The Incas often drank to the sun or poured libations intended for the sun into the earth at sacred places such as the ushnu, a ceremonial hole in the central plaza of Cuzco.

LAND OF THE DREAMING

The traditions of the Australian Aborigines are rich in myth and ritual. From earliest times, they have remained in sacred contact with the natural world, regarding their land as the embodiment of both human beings and gods.

UNTIL THE ARRIVAL OF THE EUROPEANS in the late 18th century, the Aboriginal culture of Australia had remained uninterrupted by conquest or invasion for about 25,000 years. This provided the Aborigines with an immensely long period in which they could study and adapt to their environment. Thus they came to conclude that the natural world embodied profound metaphysical principles relevant to all existence. Like the peoples of other ancient cultures, they recognized, in the various natural formations of the earth, a wise, all-knowing quality that they interpreted as divine. To them, the land had to be understood to be sacred if true wisdom was to be attained. They believe that the land itself is the Great Mother, Kunapipi, provider and helpmate, ritual womb and procreator.

Such beliefs are in part derived from the land itself. Australia is an ancient continent. It is more geologically settled than topographies created more recently such

In Aboriginal belief, the Dreaming is a mythological period with a beginning but no foreseeable end.

as those of the Himalayas or the Rocky Mountains. As a result the land itself seems almost inert and is therefore believed to be permeated with a certain "power," which, the Aborigines say, can be felt by anyone who walks through it. The Aborigines call this power *djang*.

The creation of the land

To the Australian Aborigines, djang is an emanation from the Sky Heroes, the mythic creatures who made the land at the time of the Dreaming. In Aboriginal belief, the Dreaming is a mythological period with a beginning but no foreseeable end. It continues even today. Through their actions the Sky Heroes shape and humanize the natural environment. Some of the Sky Heroes were responsible for creating human life.

The Sky Heroes are eternal, it is believed. Although, in Aboriginal mythology, some of them are killed, or disappear, or are changed into natural features, such as

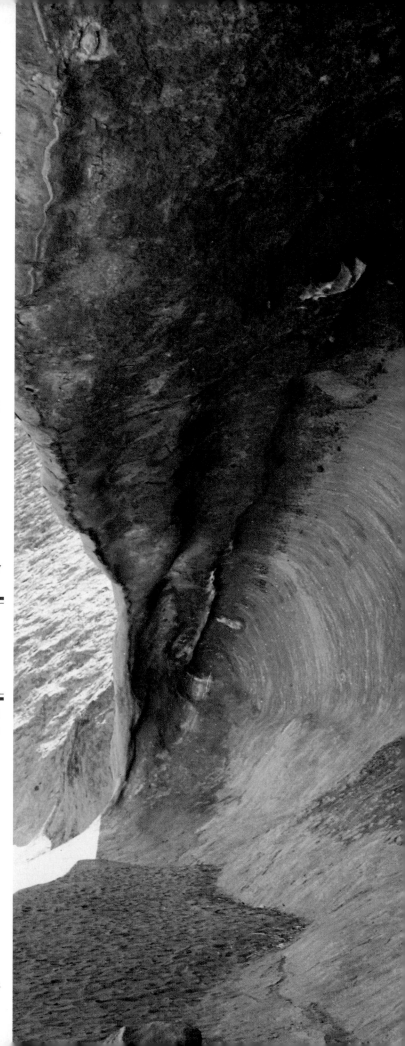

Map of Australia

PRESERVING TRADITIONS

Although Captain Cook's arrival at Botany Bay in 1770 is commonly celebrated as the official discovery of Australia, Aboriginal Australians denounce Cook as a symbol of conquest and dispossession. They argue that the continuity of Aboriginal habitation stretching back 25,000 years before that date make it one of the oldest living cultures in the world.

European influence

It has not been easy for the Aborigines to preserve their traditions. The early European settlers were mostly hostile to Aborigines and their culture, and expected both to die out. That actually happened around the southern and eastern coasts, as the Aborigines were dominated by the foreign settlers and became partly European, not only in their way of life, but also through intermarriage.

However, where European settlement was less heavy, in the central and the northern regions, and especially in the inhospitable wastes of Arnhem Land and the Western Desert, Aboriginal culture remained almost unaffected. It is in these regions that the many myths and legends surrounding the divine character of the Australian landscape survive.

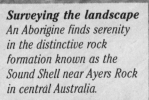

Surveying the landscape
An Aborigine finds serenity in the distinctive rock formation known as the Sound Shell near Ayers Rock in central Australia.

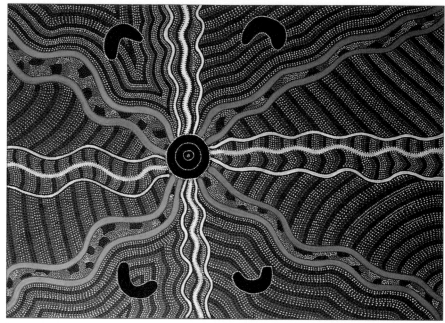

The creation of the land
This painting from Yuendemu in central Australia represents the Dreaming, the time when, according to Aboriginal lore, the land was created by mythical, godlike creatures.

Ayers Rock
The great mass of Ayers Rock in central Australia is an important totemic site for the people of the area, who call it Uluru. Many Aboriginal myths are associated with this dramatic landmark.

a rocky outcrop or a waterhole, their essential quality remains undiminished — indeed, they are considered to be as spiritually alive today as they ever were. Places where the Sky Heroes performed some action or were transformed into something else became sacred, and it is around these places that Aborigines focus their rituals.

The Rainbow Snake
The Sky Heroes may take the form of mythical animals, such as Marlu, the Great Kangaroo, or Maletji, the Law Dog. They may also be supernatural entities such as the Great Snake, or Rainbow Snake, which, known by various regional names, is a popular icon throughout Australia. But the supernatural Sky Heroes known as Wandjinas can be found only in the Kimberley region of

northwest Australia. They are depicted in local rock paintings as huge cloudlike beings with eyes but no mouths.

Thus, when an Aborigine points out a rocky outcrop and tells you it is Marlu, the Great Kangaroo, he is describing the natural feature, its iconic presence, and its mythical implication all at once. Land, Sky Hero, and myth become one.

Tribal lands embody Aboriginal beliefs — not to revere the land is to desecrate it. And to treat it outside the framework of the human and celestial predicament is to condemn the earth to a diminished existence. For example, when a piece of country loses its traditions and rituals (either by the death of its guardians or because of cultural decline), Aborigines are often reluctant to visit the area, as they regard it as "rubbish country."

Totemic lifestyle
The Australian Aborigines have devised a complex and extremely diverse ritual life to embrace all that they feel is a part of

> # Not to have a double or shadow in the world is to be condemned to an inferior existence.

them. The most poignant expression of the relationship an Aborigine has with the Dreaming is his totemic identity. A man's totem is both his alter ego and a metaphysical landmark that orients him throughout life. Not to have a double or shadow in the world is to be condemned

to an inferior existence. Being linked to the Dreaming by way of a totem is a vital part of the Aboriginal way of life.

This intensely spiritual and traditional way of life imposes a range of duties and responsibilities upon each individual. He or she must look after any family territory and care for the human and animal life that lies within its boundaries, as well as memorizing hundreds of different songs, the details of myths, dance steps, and ritual acts. Ceremony and song are thus integral parts of Aboriginal spirituality; they ensure the well-being of the land just as much as do the sun and rain.

The travels of Jarapiri

Many of the Aboriginal myths describe the travels of characters who play a creative role — naming various places, altering the form of landscape, and establishing customs. Such a "Dreaming track" runs between the mountain known as Winbaraku and the cave at Ngama in the Haast Bluff region of central Australia, northwest of Alice Springs. Winbaraku, for example, was the birthplace of Jarapiri, the Great Snake. Here, too, the First People were thought to have emerged from the earth at this time to carry the Great Snake northward. The mountain itself is made up of several Sky Heroes: Jarapiri; the Nabanunga, a group of women in love with Jarapiri; blind Jarapiri Bomba, a lesser snake who stayed behind when Jarapiri ventured north; the Wanbanbiri, or woodgall people; Mamu-boijunda, the barking spider; the hare-wallaby people known as the Jukalpi; and the Latalpa snake-women. These creatures are the world-creators that the local Walbiri people worship in their rituals and songs.

Jukuita cave

At Ngama, 70 miles north of Winbaraku, a large cave known as Jukuita sheltered Jarapiri on his Dreaming journey north to Maningrida on the coast of Arnhem Land. Ngama itself is a haven for Maletji, the mythical dog-people and law-men. In midwinter the tribesmen of the region

Maletji Law Dog
This rock painting from Western Australia is of a Maletji Law Dog. In myth, the Law Dogs were Sky Heroes who traveled across Australia, forming the landscape wherever they scratched for water. They are so named because they were believed to be responsible, at least in part, for the dissemination of Aboriginal law.

Wandjina figure
This Aboriginal rock painting of a Wandjina figure (left) was discovered in the Napier Range, Western Australia. These mouthless spirit figures are said to have helped to create the land at the time of the Dreaming. They are thought to promote rain and fertility.

Jarapiri
A painting of Jarapiri, the Great Snake, at Jukuita cave, Ngama, in central Australia. The first people to inhabit the earth are shown carrying Jarapiri on their shoulders. The photograph shows the custodians touching the snake as part of a ritual invocation.

The emergence of the snake
This rocky outcrop at Ngama is an important Aboriginal ritual center. The rock that protrudes at the bottom left represents Jarapiri emerging from the ground during his travels at the time of the Dreaming.

perform a special type of ceremony here to ensure a plentiful supply of the wild dogs that are used in hunting.

Aboriginal lore tells that at the time of the Dreaming, Jarapiri was discovered wriggling under loose sand on the floor of the cave by the Maletji. They dragged the Great Snake clear of the shelter and he curled up and went to sleep. The First People from Winbaraku met Jarapiri there and decided to perform a secret ceremony. But first they laid the Great Snake's image on the wall in the form of a painting that can be seen at the site today. On a large tableau of rock underneath an overhang Jarapiri has been brightly painted in pipeclay and red ocher, surrounded by iconic images of all the First People who had accompanied him on his mythical world-creating journeys.

After the ceremony Jarapiri slept with one of the Maletji dog-women; his semen is depicted as a white stain on the surface of the rock. A permanent supply of water in the outcrop signifies the fertile nature of Ngama, both as a drinking source for men and animals, as well as a place of inspiration for ritualized empathy with nature itself. Another aspect of the Aboriginal faith in spiritual embodiment takes the form of ritual enactment. It is a part of traditional Aboriginal belief that if a man decorates his body with the appropriate designs, he is able to mimic the actions of a specific Sky Hero. The brightly colored body of the Great Snake Jarapiri, for example, may be recreated

Animal transformation
An Aboriginal man is painted with the symbol of the Great Rainbow Snake in preparation for "transformation."

> It is a part of traditional Aboriginal belief that if a man decorates his body with the appropriate designs, he is able to mimic the actions of a specific Sky Hero.

using eagle down, blood, charcoal, ocher and pipeclay. When a man is decorated in this way and singing the traditional Aboriginal songs, he is no longer himself. The act of imitation transforms him into his totemic alter ego. The man becomes a lizard, a snake, a kangaroo, or even the Great Snake Jarapiri himself. Through the mythic image, the man has taken on the persona of the sacred land from which he too was born.

Earth wisdom
Stories such as those of Jarapiri's travels are repeated throughout the whole of Australia. Before contact with the Europeans, the entire continent was considered a network of sacred places, all permeated with djang. The different myths, songs, dances, and ceremonies that were associated with each place were known to a select group of fully initiated individuals. These were occasionally shared with visitors at ritually appropriate times. Thus a spiritual fraternity existed throughout the whole of the land whose task was to celebrate its sacred nature. In turn, the land made its presence felt as a living symbol of mythical power. People and land became united by a unique and enduring bond. What they had evolved together was a body of "earth wisdom" that could be applied at times of natural or tribal crisis. For the Aborigines, the Dreaming was therefore ever-present, a supreme reality governing the lives of humans, animals, and the entire natural world.

A PARABLE FOR SURVIVAL
The author and poet James G. Cowan, who now lives in Sydney, Australia, has written a series of books about the peoples of early Australia. In *The Aborigine Tradition* (1992), Cowan suggests that the Australian Aborigines offer us all a parable for survival. Many of them cling to their rich cultural heritage, Cowan suggests, despite all attempts by modern settlers to demean it.

In Aboriginal beliefs we find a conviction that human beings are capable of much more than just a material existence. To Aborigines, the surrounding landscape is not merely an object of beauty or a provider, it is a symbol of the divine and must be handed on in the same, uncorrupted condition as it came down to them.

Exhausting resources
Cowan suggests that if we ignore Aboriginal traditions and their deep faith in the harmony of all nature, we do so at our own risk. The destruction of the ozone layer, global warming, environmental pollution, and the exhaustion of the earth's natural resources are all the result of mistreating the land. The Aborigines' message is both implicit in their culture and explicit in their campaigns for the return of their tribal lands. They want modern man to stop abusing the earth before it is too late to prevent its destruction.

SHARING THE POWER

"While I was there, the djang — that residual energy left over from the Dreaming — was ever present for me. I became aware of the extraordinary power that emanated from the mountain."

THE AUTHOR AND POET James G. Cowan has spent much of his life studying the different cultures of traditional peoples. Visiting Winbaraku, in central Australia, with its proud Aboriginal guardian, Two Bob, Cowan described how he was immediately struck by the monumentality of the place.

"Here," he explains, "was the very beginning of a powerful myth of world-creation. Like Two Bob, I was not looking at a mere mountain but at the incarnation of a celestial reality here on earth. At the time of the Dreaming, the Sky Heroes emerged from underground chambers to create Walbiri country. Here they found themselves on the featureless plain, Winbaraku. The outcome of this was the creation of the huge mountain, which in itself took the forms of the various Sky Heroes. Ever since then Two Bob and his forebears have made the journey to the mountain in order to evoke this primordial event in ritual and song."

Traditional songs

At Winbaraku, Two Bob sang the traditional Aboriginal songs that Walbiri people sing at the site. All of these sacred songs, Cowan explains, convey one basic message: at the dawn of creation a stillness prevailed throughout the whole land in which the Sky Heroes brought themselves into being. This act of self-creation was in turn monumentalized in the form of the landscape around Winbaraku. The landscape itself thus became sacred. By performing rituals at the site, the local Walbiri people believe they will attain true wisdom.

Cowan also felt an overwhelming sense of energy during his visit to Winbaraku. "While I was there, the djang — that residual energy left over from the Dreaming — was ever present for me. I became aware of the extraordinary power that emanated from the mountain. It was both an imaginative essence and a traditional icon that I could experience at one and the same time. In the process Two Bob and I had learned how to share a myth — after Two Bob had recited the songs, we were different people who now shared a common sense of resolution."

LANDSCAPES OF
THE GODDESS

Many ancient peoples worshiped a deity known as the Earth Mother, or Great Goddess. Sometimes they saw her outline in the shape of the hills and mountains of the landscape around them.

OME OF THE PEOPLES of ancient Scotland believed that certain hills represented the life-giving breasts of the Earth Mother. The island of Jura off the west coast of Scotland, for example, has a range of mountains known as the Paps, which in the local dialect means nipple. The central heights of these mountains are symmetrical and rounded, like breasts.

The Earth Mother goddess is connected not just with hills, but also with the sun. The prehistoric peoples of northern Europe believed that the sun itself was female. Alexander Thom, author of many books on megalithic sacred sites and a former professor at Oxford University,

> ## The people who created these ancient monuments envisioned the sun as a goddess returning to her place in the distant hills.

uncovered a possible connection between the sun and the hills at certain megalithic monuments in Scotland. At Ballochroy on the Kintyre Peninsula, for example, the middle stone of a row of three large menhirs was smoothed on the side facing the most northerly of the Paps of Jura, Beinn Corra, about 19 miles away. There the midsummer sun would have set more than 4,000 years ago when the stones were placed at the site.

Forty miles north is another prehistoric site, Kintraw. From this point, a sightline stretches to the Paps of Jura, which are about 27 miles to the southwest. At Kintraw, the midwinter sun would have set in the gap between two of the Paps. Perhaps the people who created these ancient monuments envisioned the sun as a goddess returning to her place in the distant hills.

Three Celtic goddesses
Throughout Western Europe, from around 1200 B.C. until the Roman invasions of the first century A.D., the Celts worshiped a triumvirate of fertility goddesses. These goddesses are believed by scholars to come from an even more ancient tradition than the gods normally worshiped by the Celts, for they assured abundant food supplies and freedom from illness.

Three deities in a frieze from Delphi c. *525* B.C.

GREAT GODDESSES

In ancient times, in the countries that bordered the Mediterranean, one goddess was worshiped above all. Known variously as Astarte, Isis, Cybele, Ishtar, Rhea, and Gaea, she was the Earth Mother, eternally fruitful and the source of all life. But by the 9th century B.C., when Homer was writing, the Earth Mother was no longer the principal deity of the ancient Greeks, who were the successors to these older traditions.

The Earth Mother goddess of Crete had three forms. One, who was probably called Rhea by the ancient Minoans, reappears in Greek mythology as the mother of the greatest of their gods, Zeus. The other two were named Dictynna and Britomartis. They were maidens, not mothers. The Greeks later referred to them jointly as the Cretan Artemis.

Fertility goddess

Aphrodite, not Rhea or Artemis, was the Greek goddess of fertility. Rather than being an all-creating mother, she ruled over the realm of love. She also governed the fertility of animals and human beings, thereby taking on some of the functions and duties of the original Earth Mother goddess.

Facing the goddess
The middle one of the three standing stones of Ballochroy in Scotland has a smoothed side that faces the sun as it sets behind the Paps of Jura. These peaks were sacred to the Earth Mother.

The Earth Mother goddess was also the principal deity of the peoples of the Aegean. She was worshiped both by the Minoans of Crete and by the Mycenaeans of the Greek mainland.

Later Celtic peoples also saw the Mother Goddess in the landscape. British scholar Dr. Anne Ross has suggested that aspects of Celtic religion and superstitions "are written into the surrounding landscape in the form of place names which persist and are archaic." For example, the name of an estuary in Wales, the Aberaeron, may derive from the name of the ancient Celtic war goddess, Aerona.

The Celtic scholar, Proinsias MacCana, writes in an anthology entitled *The Celts* (1991) that the Celts had a deep concern with the sacred geography of their land. MacCana emphasizes the importance of this "geographical dimension of religious usage" in the Celtic worldview.

A pair of rounded hills near Killarney in Ireland, known locally as the Paps of Anu, demonstrate the relationship between landscape and legend. In Irish mythology, Anu (or Danu) was the mother of the last gods to rule the earth, the Tuatha Dé Danann. According to Dr. Ross, these hills "personify the powers of the goddess embedded in the land."

Goddess of the land

In Perthshire, Scotland, traces of the cult of the goddess of the land can still be found. Several of the region's mountains are known as Beinn na Cailliche, which means "the hill of the hag-goddess." The Cailleach was the name used in Scotland for one of the three Celtic Earth Mother goddesses. These goddesses were once reputed to stalk the hills and valleys.

Remnants of belief in the Earth Mother goddess survived even after the coming of Christianity to Scotland. Many of these were recorded by Adamnan, the Irish biographer of St. Columba, who wrote in the seventh century. He mentions a river

in Perthshire known, in Latin, as *Nigra Dea*, which means "the Black Goddess." Numerous other Black Goddess rivers and lakes are found in the central Highlands.

Glen Lyon, an isolated area in the Highlands, was renowned until the 19th century for the wildness of its inhabitants and their determination to cling to their pagan ways. Many old traditions and customs were practiced in the glen until well into this century. Beltine fires were lit, and these were used to bake a special bread known as a bannock. A portion of the bread was blackened as a sacrifice, probably to the goddess herself.

The Greek landscape

The Earth Mother goddess was also the principal deity of the peoples who lived on the shores of the Aegean before the time of the ancient Greeks. The goddess was worshiped both by the Minoans of Crete and the Mycenaeans of the Greek mainland.

Vincent Scully, a professor of art history at Yale University, has uncovered evidence that the form of the Mother Goddess was also believed

Oak idol
Five feet high, her eye sockets inlaid with magical quartz pebbles, this goddess effigy was found buried in a wickerwork shrine in Scotland.

SECRETS OF THE GLEN

The goddess promised to bless the land and the stock and crops, and bring the people good luck.

AT GLEN LYON, in a remote and forgotten corner of the Scottish Highlands, one pagan tradition remains alive. An ancient shrine is still maintained by the local shepherd, who performs a simple ritual there twice a year, in accordance with the wishes of the Celtic goddess, the Cailleach.

Legend has it that a couple once came down to Glen Lyon from the hills on the evening before May Day, the Celtic feast of Beltine. They were deities: the man was huge, and the woman, who was heavily pregnant, was even bigger. The local people welcomed them, and the couple stayed until their child was born. Because of the kindness they had received, the deities blessed the spot and promised to do so forever if the correct ritual was performed each year in their memory.

A miniature house was built where they had lived, and three large water-worn stones were selected to represent them. They asked that, at Beltine, the turf roof was replaced with one of thatch. The stones were then to be washed in the nearby stream, Allt na Cailliche, before being placed at the door of the house to watch over the glen all summer long. At the Celtic new year, which was known as Samain, on November 1, a new turf roof was to be put on, any cracks sealed up, and the figures placed inside the house. The entrance was then sealed for the winter, and a large white quartz stone that could be seen from the hills was placed on the roof.

Blessed by the goddess

If these things were done each year, the Cailleach promised to bless the land and the stock and crops, and bring the people good luck. Even today, the shepherd still carries on the old tradition, and the glen remains under the protection of the Great Goddess who once found shelter there.

Minoan bull ritual
A fresco painted c.1700–1450 B.C., from the Minoan palace of Knossos, shows a youth about to leap over the horns of a bull. This act had religious significance since the bull was the emblem of the Great God of the Minoans.

Minoan ax
This golden double ax, called a labrys, was found in a cave on Crete, and was made around 1500 B.C.

to be visible in the landscape of ancient Greece and of Crete. A mountain range that can be seen from Poros in Greece is described locally as a woman lying on her back. In his book *The Earth, the Temple, and the Gods* (1962), Scully described the line of the hills: "the head low on the north, a long neck, high breasts, arched stomach, long legs with the knees drawn up." It may be significant that Aphrodite, the goddess of love and fertility of the later Greeks, who took on some of the functions of the Mother Goddess, has a shrine nearby.

Mountains of the goddess
One symbol of the Earth Mother goddess that recurs time and again in association with the temples of ancient Crete is the horned, or cleft, mountain. Scully states that "The landscape and the temples together form the architectural whole." He also claims that the cleft or saddle-peaked mountain was seen as a goddess symbol because it echoes the contours of her breasts, hips, and upraised arms. This shape is repeated in many different Minoan ceremonial objects that have been found by archeologists on Crete.

Entire palaces contain clues to the goddess's importance: the courtyard of the palace of Knossos on Crete opens out to the distant cleft peak of Mount Juktas. The *propylaia*, or entrance, is oriented

Twin peaks
From the Acropolis in Athens, Mount Hymettos can be seen in the distance. Its twin peaks may have inspired the Greek fascination with horn imagery.

directly toward the mountain. At Gournia the palace points to two hills, which are so close together and so rounded that, according to Scully, they resemble not horns but the breasts of the goddess. Other Cretan palaces associated with horned mountains are Mallia, which is near Mount Dikte, and Phaistos, which aligns to Mount Ida.

Horn-shaped artifacts

The Minoan culture of Crete left many artifacts indicative of their worship of the Mother Goddess. For example, stylized clay or stone bull's horn shapes, called

> ## In outdoor arenas beneath the mountain, young men and women would seize the horns of a charging bull and leap over its back.

sacral horns, were found in many of the Cretan palaces. Another image that was repeatedly inscribed on palace walls, on ritual columns, and in figurines, was that of the *labrys*, a highly stylized version of the Minoan ritual double ax. The outline of this shape, like the horns, resembles the basic crescent form of the cleft or horned-peak mountains.

The Minoan bull ritual may have been connected to the horned-peak symbolism. In outdoor arenas beneath the mountains, young men and women would seize the horns of a charging bull and leap over its back. The shape of the bulls' horns is repeated in such Minoan religious objects as the sacral horns and the curving labrys.

Goddesses with raised arms

The upraised arms of many Minoan goddess figurines also form the familiar crescent shape, as do the much smaller Mycenaean terra-cotta goddess figurines. Elsewhere in the Mediterranean, tomb slabs from the Castelluccio cemetery in Sicily were carved into a crude depiction of a female figure with upraised arms, breasts, and head, while many items of

Snake goddess
This faience figurine from Knossos holds two snakes that symbolize fertility. Her upraised arms and breasts form a crescent or horned shape that is often associated with the Earth Mother goddess.

With arms upraised
The great Egyptian goddess Isis is shown with upraised arms in this relief from a tomb.

pottery from Sicily, the Lipari Islands to its north, and southern Italy, possess "horned" handles depicting a stylized goddess figure with upraised arms.

This motif was obviously of great significance, since it occurs in numerous different ancient cultures — the female figures of predynastic Egypt, for instance, are invariably depicted with upraised arms. The German Jungian psychologist Erich Neumann believes that this gesture, which is so universally associated with the Earth Mother, might indicate prayer, invocation, or the conjuring of the deity.

THE ANCIENT MOUND BUILDERS

The eastern half of the United States is dotted with thousands of huge earthworks built long ago. Many are in the shape of animals or humans. Archeologists are learning more about the people who built them, but much of the symbolism and ritual function of these extraordinary earthworks remains a mystery.

IT WAS A CLEAR, crisp day in the autumn of 1976. American sociology professor Robert Harner stood on top of the mysterious Serpent Mound in Adams County, Ohio, and looked out along the length of the 1,348-foot-long coiled earthwork. As he did so, he was suddenly shaken by "the coldest, most abject terror I have ever experienced." Feeling an evil force moving toward him, Prof. Harner saw it outlined in a pattern of swirling leaves. As the leaves moved closer, Harner was so horrified by the sight that he nearly fainted.

Suddenly, as quickly as it had arrived, the "force" disappeared. The leaves fell to the ground and lay still. Harner hurried back to his car and promised himself that he would never return to the huge 2,500-year-old

Feeling an evil force moving toward him, Harner saw it outlined in a pattern of swirling leaves.

effigy mound. Later, writing about his eerie experience in *Fate* magazine (June 1977), he concluded: "Perhaps they built their mound on that particular hill because very special things happen there."

Origins of the mounds

The huge Serpent Mound that so terrified Robert Harner is just one of the thousands of curious earthworks that are dotted throughout the eastern half of the United States. They include earthworks, called effigy mounds, fashioned in the shapes of various animals, humans, and other figures. At several sites, a row of such effigies can be found, forming hilltop processions of panthers, bears, lizards, turtles, or giant birds. Far from being the product of a single, uniform culture, the mounds and earthworks were apparently created at various times — from as long ago as 500 B.C. to as recently as A.D 1500 — by several American Indian societies. Were the mounds ancient places of worship or celebration? Or were they something much more mysterious? Archeologists are

Mound excavation
This 1850 painting by the Irish-American artist John Egan shows the explorer Dr. Montroville Dickeson and workers excavating a burial mound in Louisiana, Mississippi. The painting shows the layers of the mound and the skeletons lying in place.

WHO WERE THE MOUND BUILDERS?

The first American mounds were discovered by the explorers and settlers who began to spread out across America in the late 1700's and early 1800's. Most authorities were baffled by the mounds. Their apparent antiquity, the incredible planning that must have gone into their construction, and the lack of local knowledge on the subject, led to fanciful speculations about the identity of their builders. Some people believed that they were built by the 10 Lost Tribes of Israel, the Vikings, or even the Atlanteans. Others claimed they were built by a long-vanished superior race. One such pundit, the 19th-century investigator Caleb Atwater, noted insultingly that the mounds "owe their origin to a people far more civilized than our Indians."

The president's proof

Others had less fanciful ideas. Even in the 1700's some people claimed the builders were American Indians. Among these was the third president of the United States, Thomas Jefferson. Around 1780, Jefferson excavated one of the mounds near his home in central Virginia and estimated that it contained more than 1,000 American Indian skeletons.

Seip Mound
Seip Mound in Ohio may have been the burial place of an ancient Indian royal family. Excavation in the late 19th century yielded the skeletons of four adults and two children, as well as copper, mica, silver, tortoiseshell ornaments, and thousands of pearls.

105

A SHAMANIC LINK

The shamans of the American Indians entered trance states, during which the spirit body was thought to leave the physical body and undergo magical flight. Because numerous ancient effigy mounds depicted winged creatures, some researchers have suggested that the effigy mounds are linked to shamanism. A belief in man-animal transformations is shared by nearly all American Indians; so, too, is the idea that sacred animals can instruct people through dreams or trances. The depictions of birds and winged animals may have symbolized the flight of the shaman.

Copper mushroom

Some of the artifacts found at effigy mounds and other earthworks also suggest a link with the out-of-body sensation associated with shamanic flight. At the major Hopewell Indian site of Mound City, Ohio, an object of wood and copper in the shape of a mushroom was found at the center of a burial mound. This may have represented the fly agaric mushroom, known to have been used in shamanic rituals for its hallucinogenic properties.

still searching for the key that will help them unlock the mystery of these puzzling remnants from a vanished past.

Prehistoric American Indians traditionally buried their dead with the objects they valued most. Examination of the many thousands of artifacts that have been discovered within the earthworks has provided a partial picture of the people who built them. After years of classifying their finds, most archeologists now agree that there were three distinct mound-building cultures, which, despite the sophistication of the monuments they left behind, were no more advanced than any other tribes of their times. These were the Adena, the Hopewell, and the Mississippian Indians.

The Adena

The earliest of the mound builders, the Adena, flourished between 500 B.C. and A.D. 200 in Ohio. They are credited with building the largest and most famous of the effigy mounds, the Serpent Mound in Ohio, some 2,500 years ago. This huge embankment of rocks, earth, and clay is four feet high, 20 feet wide, and more than 1,300 feet long. Inside the serpent's open jaws is an oval object, thought by many to represent an egg. Some people believe the mound may have been built to celebrate some astronomical event; others see it as an ancient symbol of the earth spirit.

Sun-watching complex
A reconstruction of the Cahokia complex as it may have looked during Mississippian occupancy (A.D. 800–1500). Some researchers believe the complex was built in such a way to observe solar events. The huge Monks Mound can be seen at its center.

The Adena were most noted, however, for their elaborate burial customs. The dead were often buried with a wide assortment of objects, such as bracelets, beads, stone tablets, and masks. Bodies were placed in log tombs that were then burned and covered with earth. Over the years, as more bodies were added, the mounds grew larger and higher. In time the Adena erected circular enclosures around their mounds.

From its heartland in southern Ohio, Adena influence spread west into Indiana, south into Kentucky, and as far east as Maryland and New York. Some researchers estimate that the total number of Adena mound sites in this region is between 300 and 500. But by the first century A.D., Adena culture began to wane and Hopewell culture to develop. The Adena and Hopewell were not different races of people, they were merely different societies with different customs. It seems that the Hopewell style simply became more fashionable.

The Hopewell

The Hopewell style was a grander version of the Adena; the earthworks were more extravagant and the burial gifts within them more luxurious. From around 100 B.C. to A.D. 350, the Hopewell culture spread from the Ohio Valley throughout much of the eastern half of the United

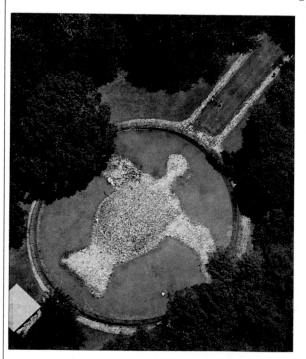

Magical flight
This effigy mound in Georgia is attributed to the Mississippian Indians. Made from rocks embedded in earth, the mound is in the form of a huge flying eagle, which may have been symbolic of shamanic flight.

States. As well as their huge geometric earthworks, which combined a variety of different shapes such as circles, squares and octagons, the Hopewell people also built effigy burial mounds. In the upper Mississippi Valley, which runs through Illinois, Minnesota, Wisconsin, and Iowa, the Hopewell built mounds in the shape of humans, birds, and animals. Bodies were often buried where the heart of the animal or person represented would be.

Magical flight

Many of these figures could only be fully appreciated from the air, suggesting, some people claim, that the Hopewell Indians may have practiced levitation or experienced out-of-body sensations. The effigy mounds, especially those depicting winged creatures, were thought to be symbols of this "magical flight." Beneath many of the earthen burial mounds, the 19th-century researchers E. G. Squier and E. H. Davis found enormous, well-built structures, which were used not only for housing the bodies of the dead but for all the complex preparations for burial.

Ancient American Indians thought that communication with the spirit world was possible through dreams, trances,

---

> ## Effigy mounds, especially those depicting winged creatures, were thought to be symbols of shamanic "magical flight."

---

and symbolic transformations into sacred animals, all of which were believed to be important aspects of shamanism. A large number of Hopewell burial mounds have yielded animal skin costumes and masks, suggesting, some claim, a strong link with shamanic spiritual transformations.

Throughout the 4th and 5th centuries, the Hopewell culture began to decline and Indian burial practices eventually became much simpler. The reasons for these changes are not understood.

The Mississippians

In the centuries following the decline of the Hopewell culture, social priorities began to change, and around the start of the 9th century, the last of the mound builders, the Mississippians, started to emerge. By A.D. 1500 the culture had spread west and southeast from the central Mississippi Valley as far as Texas and Florida.

Unlike the Adena and the Hopewell, the Mississippians appear to have built many of their mounds for purposes other than burial. In many towns and villages they built high palisades and flat-topped rectangular earthworks that served as bases for temples, meetinghouses, and other important buildings.

The Mississippians buried most of their dead in cemeteries, yet the earlier burial mounds did not entirely disappear. In larger burial sites, the Mississippian elite were interred in special burial mounds with elaborate gifts reflecting their status. Excavation of some of the mounds has revealed numerous skeletons and a variety of grave goods.

The Cahokia mounds

One of the first, and the largest, ancient Mississippian settlement, Cahokia (located near what is now St. Louis, Missouri), contained 100 or more mounds, and including its outskirts, covered 125 square miles. By some estimates it was home to as many as 40,000 people. Its centerpiece, Monks Mound, is the largest prehistoric earthen construction in the world.

Research suggests that many of the mounds in Cahokia are oriented to the cardinal directions and may have been used, in conjunction with posts set in the ground, to mark astronomical events.

The decline of the mound builders

By the early 15th century the great Mississippian settlements had begun to decline. The people who had built the mounds did not disappear, but their societies broke down and they returned to a simpler way of life.

An ancient portrait
This face embossed on copper was found at a Mississippian burial mound. Dating from c. A.D. 1000, it shows details of hairstyle and facial decoration typical of the Mississippian culture.

BURIED TREASURE

Scholars and archeologists have been trying to solve the mystery of who built the great burial mounds of North America since the 1800's. The best clues may lie hidden within the mounds themselves.

Grave Creek Mound

MOUND EXCAVATION

This etching shows the method of excavation, in 1838, of the Grave Creek Mound in the Ohio Valley. A shaft was made from the apex of the mound to the base (b to a), and this was then intersected at the base by a horizontal shaft (a to e). The diagram shows the two burial chambers within the mound, one at the base (a), and another 30 feet above (c). The lower chamber contained two skeletons and the upper chamber contained one. In addition to these remains, the excavators found thousands of shell beads, many mica ornaments, several copper bracelets, and various articles carved in stone.

I N THE 1930'S, THE BURIAL MOUND known as Craig Mound in the huge Mississippian center of Spiro in eastern Oklahoma was practically hollowed out by looters. They escaped with copper breastplates and masks, magnificently engraved shell cups, ornate stone figures, and wooden mortuary carvings. The haul was one of such unparalleled richness that newspaper stories describing the theft referred to the 1,000-year-old burial mound as "King Tut's Tomb."

Archeologists attempting to salvage what remained of the Spiro site found a great mortuary for the elite. Many of the burial mounds were heaped with personal possessions and gifts, providing clues to the wealth and status of the Mississippian culture.

Secrets of the dead

The Spiro site was not the only one found to contain such artifacts. Most of the mounds that have been excavated by archeologists have revealed an amazing array of tools, weapons, jewelry, and ornaments accompanying the bones of the dead. Not only have these articles helped to identify the different mound-building cultures, but they are often the only clues researchers have to the social, economic, and religious practices of these people.

Hidden weapons
This dart point is one of the thousands of objects found at numerous burial sites in the valleys of the Ohio and Mississippi rivers. Dating from 500 B.C. to A.D. 500, the dart points are believed to belong to the Hopewell culture.

Most of the mounds that have been excavated have revealed an amazing array of tools, weapons, jewelry, and ornaments accompanying the bones of the dead.

Shell pendant

Shamanic animals
A shell pendant, found in a Mississippian burial mound, shows a panther attacking a bird of prey. These creatures were commonly represented in the shape of effigy mounds, and some researchers believe they are symbols of shamanic transformation.

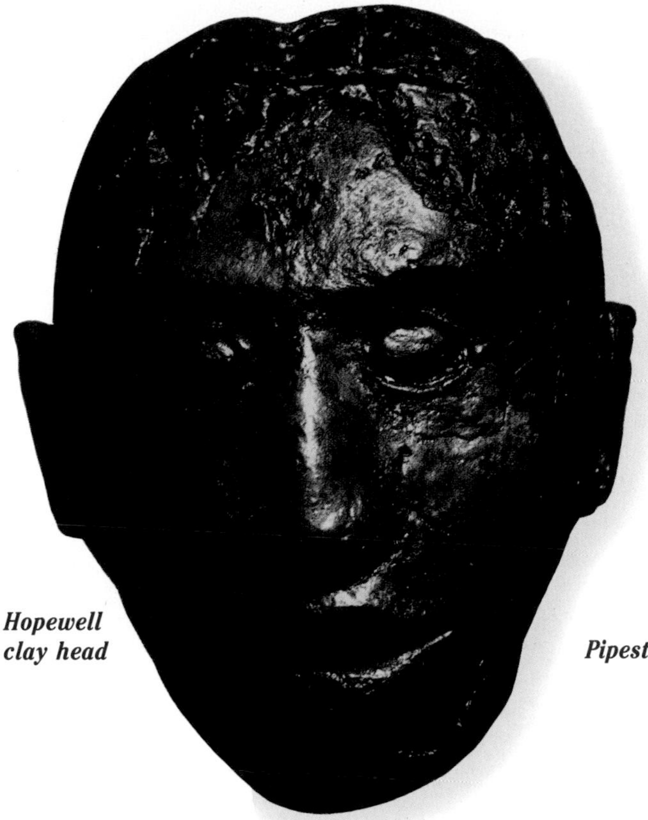

*Hopewell
clay head*

Ceremonial pipe

This 8-inch-tall pipestone effigy was found in 1901 in the Ohio Valley, the heartland of the Adena culture (*c.* 500 B.C.–A.D. 200). Smoking had religious overtones for ancient Indians; such elaborate pipes were used for ceremonial smoking only.

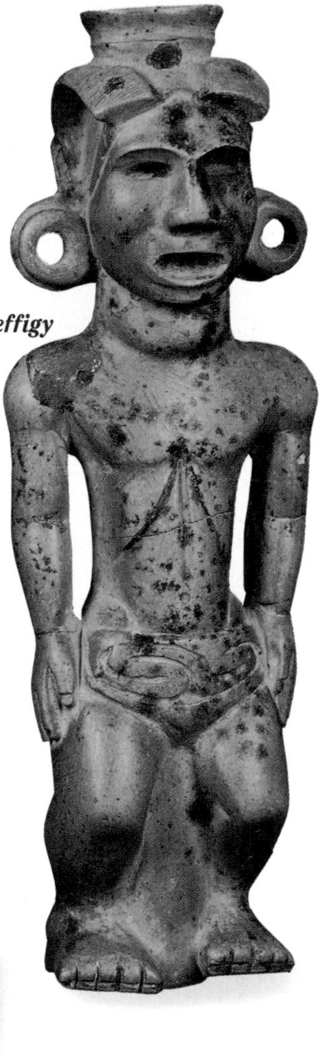

Pipestone effigy

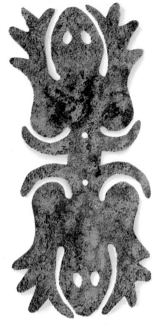

Copper frog

A twin frog copper effigy found in a Hopewell burial mound in Newark, Ohio. The Hopewell Indians fashioned many ornaments from the copper they found on the shores of Lake Superior.

Death's mask

This clay head, found in an Ohio Hopewell mound, is said to be associated with a death cult. Some researchers suggest that the Hopewell Indians built their burial mounds for important members of their society, and that other humans were sacrificed and buried along with them to act as servants.

Sandstone engraving

Fine work

This detailed mica ornament in the shape of a bear is just one of the thousands of different treasures found at various Ohio burial mounds. Attributed to the Hopewell people, such designs help to rank them among the great artisans of the Americas.

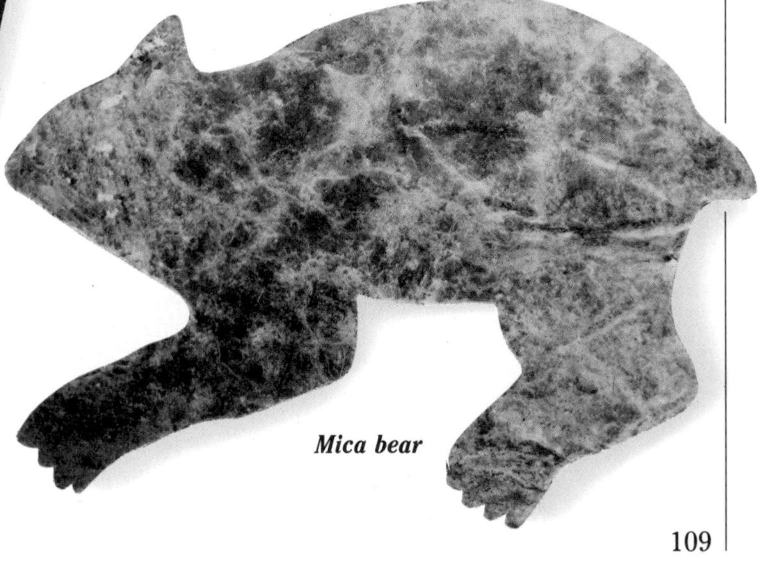

Burial bird

An abstract sandstone engraving from Ohio depicts a bird of prey, a motif that is thought to have been associated with burial — bodies were sometimes placed outdoors, where birds of prey would strip the bones of flesh before interment.

Mica bear

SECRETS OF THE
JAPANESE LANDSCAPE

In Japan, where the Shinto religion has been practiced for centuries, many places, such as mountains, islands, and caves, are believed to be holy and are revered.

CENTRAL TO THE SHINTO RELIGION is a strong sense of the holiness of nature. The Japanese landscape is studded with a variety of local shrines, built at the places where their forebears perceived some spiritual presence: on mountains, next to sacred stones, or near bodies of running water such as rivers or streams.

The Shinto religion began before the time of written history in Japan as a collection of loosely related local traditions. Shinto beliefs and traditions were eventually written down in the 8th century A.D., and the ancient religion has changed very little since.

The powers of nature

The basis of Shinto is a spiritual presence known as *kami*, which has many meanings including "god" and "spirit." It can describe a sacred presence or simply the powers of nature. Kami may take any one of a number of forms, including that of trees, stones, caves, springs, waterfalls, islands, and especially mountains.

Places and objects that are believed to be full of kami are marked by a twist of straw rope. In addition, animals such as snakes and foxes may be messengers of kami or occasionally forms taken on by kami. Although the variety of meanings that the term kami can have and the many things that are said to have kami can be bewildering, this sense of the sacred permeating the natural world is a common feature of ancient religious beliefs.

Sacred mountains

Mount Miwa, near Nara, is thought to be the oldest shrine in Japan. This holy hill embodies kami. People who wish to climb the mountain must first purify

themselves at the shrine at the foot of the mountain, both to spiritually prepare to appreciate the sanctity of the place and to protect the sacredness of the mountain itself. Many of the boulders and trees that can be seen on the way up the mountainside have been garlanded with twists of straw, indicating concentrations of kami — in this case, the spirit presence of the mountain.

But the sacredness of this mountain goes further: it forms an alignment with other sacred hills. The winter solstice sun, associated in Japan with ancestor worship, sets behind Unchiyama, a holy hill a few miles away.

Tatetsuki
An important prehistoric center of ritual, Tatetsuki stands on a low hill and includes a stone circle and avenue, a burial mound, and a stone carved with wavy lines. It was built nearly 2,000 years ago.

The alignments of sacred places in Japan are not as precise as the leys found by Alfred Watkins in England. They are broad, loose alignments of sacred sites that may be two miles wide. Paul Devereux in *The Ley Hunter's Companion* (1979) coined the term "geomantic corridor" to describe this imprecise type of alignment.

Mount Fuji
The highest and most sacred mountain in Japan, Fuji has a shrine at its peak that thousands of pilgrims visit each year.

One such alignment can be seen from the ancient stone circle built on the hill of Tatetsuki in southeastern Japan. At one time the circle was paved with pebbles, and a stone avenue led off it. Archeologists believe that

---

As the sun rises behind Mount Shinto, a line is lit from the ancient heart of Japan to the far west.

---

the huge stones themselves may have been colored red, perhaps indicating an ancient belief in the Earth Mother or in some sort of primitive earth magic.

In the third century A.D. two people were buried within the stone circle, one with full ritual trappings, including an iron sword (which may have symbolized earthly power), sacred *magatama* ("comma-shaped") beads, and clay dolls, perhaps implying religious or mystical skills. Like many ancient graves, this one is floored with red ocher (clay colored with hematite or iron peroxide). Since red is the color of blood, and hence of life and strength, the red ocher may have been thought to give the dead strength for their spiritual journey to the underworld. Near the graves a stone carved with an interlacing pattern of wavy lines was unearthed. It resembles stones found in other countries known as omphalos stones, which were believed to mark the very center of the world.

A sacred gate
The gateway to a sacred natural site is known in Japan as a torii. *This torii stands off the shore of Itsukushima, an island sacred to the goddess of love, Benzaiten.*

The way of the sun

At dawn on the spring or autumn equinox, from within the stone circle at the top of the mound at Tatetsuki, the *taiyo-no-michi* (which means "way of the sun") can be seen. As the sun rises behind Mount Shinto, its rays gradually illuminate the stone circle on top of the mound, then reach on to Mount Saku in the west and beyond. By stages a line is lit from the ancient heart of Japan in the Nara plain to the far west of the country.

CHAPTER FIVE

SPIRIT LINES

Archeologists, astronomers, and other researchers have pondered the significance of the different types of straight landscape lines found all over the world. Over the years, various explanations have been offered, some mundane, some plausible, and many bizarre.

What are known as landscape lines exist in a variety of forms around the world. They include not only ley lines — tracks that follow alignments of ancient sacred sites — but also rows of standing stones, such as the Merrivale stones in England, and a number of huge designs carved onto the landscape, such as the Nazca desert lines in Peru. Concerning such remarkable creations, one question is almost always asked: Why did diverse peoples in many different places spend so much time and

FENG-SHUI

The idea that straight lines encourage the movement of spirits, while curved lines hinder them, has a parallel in the ancient art of *feng-shui*. The Chinese believe that the landscape has an energy, known as *chi*, that flows along certain lines. The art of divining these lines and managing them for the general benefit of mankind is known as feng-shui.

The flow of chi at the site of a building, for example, is all-important: too little means that the structure may be weakened and the activities performed there may be ineffectual; too much creates danger. The flow of chi to a building can be inhibited by such construction features as fountains or walls. These obstacles serve the same purpose as the curved lines or gates that are used in other cultures to hamper the progress of spirits.

Bank balance
The Bank of Credit and Commerce International in Hong Kong was not designed according to feng-shui principles. Local people were therefore not surprised when the banking group collapsed in 1991.

energy making lines in the landscape? Researchers have been asking this question since the 18th century when the discoverer of the massive and ancient English landscape feature known as the Stonehenge cursus, antiquarian William Stukeley, first theorized that a cursus was a Roman racetrack. Many less mundane theories for the landscape lines have been put forward since that time.

Straight line theories

In this century, Alfred Watkins's theory that the mysterious landscape lines in Britain are leys, old straight tracks made by the prehistoric Celtic peoples, has been perhaps the most durable of the popular theories. The idea has since been taken up by other earth mysteries enthusiasts who have embellished it with their own pet theories. Some researchers claim that leys are lines of energy. Others believe that the alleged energy can be tapped by extraterrestrial spacecraft, which use the lines to refuel before returning to their home planet.

Scholars reject such absurd theories. They prefer to rely on evidence from the past to try to determine the function of any lines on the landscape. Archeology, anthropology, and astronomy are just some of the disciplines that have provided evidence of the ways these straight lines may have been used by the people who created them.

One theory that has recently gained considerable support among researchers is that the mysterious lines that crossed the ancient landscapes were what might be called spirit lines — straight lines along which spirits were believed to travel. The theory has been developed by British earth mysteries researcher Paul Devereux in his book *Shamanism and the Mystery Lines* (1992). Evidence that Devereux has culled from archeological and anthropological sources suggests

> **The mysterious lines that crossed the ancient landscapes were spirit lines — straight lines along which spirits were believed to travel.**

that this ancient linking of spirits and lines may be a part of shamanic tradition.

Shamans were magicians, the only members of the tribe who were able to intercede with the spirit world in order to gain special knowledge and powers. To do this, the shaman, who was usually male, would go into a trance, during which his "spirit body" would become separated from his physical body. These journeys of the disembodied spirit were known as magical flights.

It is now thought by some researchers that the ancients transposed this concept of magical flight onto the landscape in the form of straight lines of various kinds. Flight is, of course, the straightest way over the land — hence the popular saying "straight as an arrow." Arrows themselves were common symbols of shamanic flight.

The landscape lines, whether on the Nazca pampas or the British countryside, may have been guides for shamanic flight. Yet the peoples who made these lines died out centuries ago and left no written record, so it is not possible to know for certain what they intended the lines to represent.

Spirit paths

The belief that spirits traveled in straight lines was widespread in northern Europe. Folklore and superstition provide many examples of this belief.

The Celts believed that fairy paths ran in straight lines from one prehistoric hill to another. It was therefore considered bad luck to build one's house on a fairy path because to do so would curtail the travels of fairies and sprites. In his book *The Middle Kingdom* (1959), Dermot MacManus recounted the story of how one Irishman began to experience poltergeist-like disturbances at one end of the new house he had built. A local wise woman told him that a corner of his house was blocking a fairy path and that the only cure was to remove the offending corner. When the man heeded her advice, the strange disturbances at his house reportedly ceased.

The witch's flight
A 19th-century watercolor showing a witch flying on her broom may be a reference to a much older belief in shamanic flight.

In Russia fishermen once ran around stone labyrinths on the shoreline of the Baltic sea. The idea was to prevent any trolls (whose mischief might bring foul weather) from following them on board their boats, by trapping them in the turns and twists of the maze. Similar stone labyrinths can still be seen on the shores of Scandinavia. Indonesian temples have low walls inside their gates to block the paths of spirits wishing to enter.

Peoples as various as the Celts of Britain, the Aborigines of Australia, the Plains Indians of North America, and the Kogi Indians of South America, believed that straight lines, whether in the form of landscape lines, roads, or even stretched threads, facilitated the movement of spirits. Other peoples thought that spirit movement could be impeded by twisting the lines or blocking their paths.

Keeping the lines open

But building straight lines along which the spirits could travel or removing any obstacles that stood in their way was not always believed to be sufficient to aid the spirits in their flight. Sometimes the lines themselves were actually swept to keep them clear. Northern European lore describes a special "spirit flail" made from branches tied with willow bark. This device was used to sweep unwanted spirits from old pathways. The Andean Indians of South America ritually swept a line or strip of ground. This was considered to be a symbolic way of creating sacred space. Some researchers believe that the spectacular

Indian lines, such as the pampa lines of Nazca, Peru, may have been swept for similar reasons in ancient times.

The shamanic tradition

The Indians in North America had a strong tradition of shamanic awareness. Over 12,000 years ago, these people migrated from central Asia, one of the heartlands of shamanism. They brought shamanic traditions with them, and these traditions survived, at least until the Europeans arrived.

In a research paper published in 1977, anthropologist Marlene Dobkin de Rios, of California State University, suggested that American landscape lines might have been created by tribal peoples under the direction of their shamans. Shamans, in

Spirit helpers
This Eskimo drawing depicts the shaman in flight accompanied by various animals, who aid him on his spiritual journey.

ALTERED STATES

Some American Indian tribes practiced vision questing to gain or increase their spiritual powers. Isolation at a sacred site, fasting, and exposure to intense heat were some of the methods used to induce visions.

In some tribes vision questing is a rite of passage while in others it is used to connect the individual with the spirit world at various important times in his life, such as when a child is to be named.

Fasting fish

This 19th-century Eskimo mask represents the soul of the salmon. Salmon fasted on their journey upstream to spawn, as did people in search of visions. Salmon were therefore thought by some tribes to be a symbol of the vision quest.

some cases, are known to have taken a variety of plant hallucinogens as part of their religious rituals. Some of the drugs reportedly induced a sensation of flight, and Dobkin de Rios has suggested that the American landscape lines may have been associated with an "aerial journey" experienced by a shaman while in a trance. It is interesting to note that some of the designs in the landscape can only be fully appreciated from the air.

Flying shamans

Dobkin de Rios has also suggested that these lines might have been associated with the American effigy mounds that were created hundreds of years ago by the Hopewell, Adena, and Mississippian peoples. The fact that many of these effigy mounds depict birds and winged humans, which so often symbolized shamanism, gives some support to this theory. Eagle feathers, especially when attached to sticks, were also a symbol of magical flight. Some Mississippian pottery is decorated with a variety of human-bird figures that were believed to represent the flying shaman.

The apparent age of such bird imagery is underscored by a 25,000-year-old Paleolithic cave painting at Lascaux, France. This painting portrays an apparently entranced

Shamanic symbolism

This Huichol yarn painting from the southwestern U.S. shows shamanic symbols such as an arrow and a stag that appears to be speaking.

man wearing an ancient bird-mask. Near him is a short stick supporting a bird's head, which was a symbol of trance in Siberia up until recent centuries.

Many other cultures show evidence of shamanic bird imagery. The Hopewell Indian shaman hung bird claw shapes

---

Bird symbolism was often associated with spirit flight throughout the ancient world.

---

cut out of mica on his ceremonial robes. Chinese Taoist priests were commonly known as "feather scholars," probably denoting their shamanic origins; and geese figure prominently in Eskimo tales of magical flight. Throughout Ireland, Celtic Druidism was also associated with magical flight. In one Irish legend, *The Siege of Druim Damhghaire*, the Druid Mog Ruith is described as wearing an *enchennach* ("bird dress") and rising into the air. Clearly, bird symbolism was often associated with spirit flight throughout the ancient world.

The flying buck

Southern African San (Bushman) rock art often depicts magical flight in the form of a figure known to archeologists as a "flying buck." Essentially an antelope with its legs raised, the flying buck is usually shown with long lines trailing

▶ PAGE 118

HEALING LINES

The ancient association between spirits and straight lines is not limited to ley alignments and other landscape lines. In many cultures, threads, ropes, and cords have spiritual significance.

IN MANY CULTURES throughout the world, threads, ropes, or cords were thought to serve as roads for the travels of spirits, wrote British researcher Paul Devereux in his 1992 book *Shamanism and the Mystery Lines*. The Australian Aborigines, for example, speak of a group of heavenly beings called the *Rai*, who travel through the sky on invisible ropes. The Aborigines believe that the Rai are spirits of the dead, and that only those people with magical powers can see the ropes they use. They also believe that during *miruru*, their name for the out-of-body state, a magical thread links the physical body and the spirit body, providing a route by which the spirit can return to the body.

This concept also exists in the beliefs of the Rigo people of Papua New Guinea. The Rigos claim that when a person has an out-of-body experience, a fishing line is attached to the spirit and remains taut as it makes its aerial journey. According to the Rigo, the line allows the spirit to return, ensuring that it does not become separated from the body indefinitely.

Thread roads

Since prehistoric times, shamanic rituals were an important part of the traditions of the Tungus people of eastern Siberia. After the Russian Revolution in 1917, most of these practices disappeared as the Tungus communities were dispersed. Until that time, however, the original ideas and practices remained virtually unchanged. In Siberia, the Tungus shaman would poke poles, to which cords were attached, through the smoke hole of his tent. The cords were then linked to sacred objects outside the tent. The spirits were believed to travel along the cord "road" into the tent, where they would share their special knowlege with the shaman. When the Tungus people of Manchuria, in

Hanging by a thread

These wooden carvings, representing shamans of the Chukchee Indian tribe, are designed to hang on threads that may symbolize the tenuous link between the body and the spirit as it pursues its magical flight.

northern China, initiated a shaman, they would attach one end of a rope or thong made of red Chinese silk or red-colored sinews to a tree. The other end was then attached to the place where the initiate sat during the three-day ceremony. "This is the road," Mircea Eliade wrote in his 1951 book *Shamanism*, "along which the spirits move." The Tungus people believed that the spirits entered the world via the tree, traveled along the silk rope, and whispered their secrets to the would-be shaman.

Releasing illness

Such spirit thread lore became particularly associated with healing. An Aboriginal healer, for example, will attach the long, thin thread made by a certain insect to the head of a sick person, and run the thread to a nearby bush where the soul of the sufferer is thought to be lodged. The long thread supposedly allows the person's soul to travel back into his or her body, making that person whole again and ending the illness.

The Buryat shamans of Siberia would position an arrow, itself a symbol of magical flight, on the ground alongside the head of a sick person and lay a red thread in a straight line from the point of the arrow to a pole erected outside the tent. The pole symbolized the world tree, by which the person's spirit entered the spirit world. This arrangement was believed to provide a route along which the soul could return to the body.

Trapping spirits

According to northern European folklore, threads could be used to block the movement of evil spirits. "Spirit traps" were made by stretching long red threads across a large hoop, mounting it on a staff, and placing it on the path that the evil spirit was supposed to haunt. The spirit, unable to pass through the taut threads, was forced to return to the spirit world.

behind it. Recent research, confirmed by the San themselves, suggests that this image relates to the shamanic out-of-body experience they undergo when trance dancing. As American mythologist Joseph Campbell says, the flying buck represents "the released soul of the trance dancers as well as the souls of the dead." In trance, the souls of the dancers "fly forth and about."

Even modern Western societies retain cultural images of this shamanic magical flight: Father Christmas flying in his reindeer-drawn sleigh through the magic midwinter night sky may derive from the ancient shamanic practices of Arctic Europe and Siberia, where the tribespeople were reindeer herders.

The Enlightened Ones
The theory that the mysterious landscape lines relate to the travels of spirits has been supported by studies of the Kogi Indians of northern Colombia. These people have remained isolated from the European influx into South America, and their culture may be the last to reflect accurately the civilization that existed before Columbus arrived in 1492. The Kogi are ruled by shaman-priests called Mamas, or Enlightened Ones, who profess to be able to see the spirit world, which they call *aluna*, even as they see the physical world. The Kogi also have mysterious pathways that crisscross their territory, linking ancient towns.

Map of the spirit world
Some of the lines incised on this Kogi standing stone map the physical paths of their territory; others show the spirit ways known to the Kogi priests, the Mamas.

Alan Ereira was the first filmmaker allowed into the Kogi's hidden mountain territory. While making his BBC documentary *The Heart of the World* (1991), he saw members of the tribe carefully sweeping one of the paved pathways under the guidance of a number of Mamas. The pathway ran up from a river in a straight line and disappeared beneath a building in one of the Kogi villages. The Mamas carefully explained to Ereira that the paved pathway was the physical trace of a spirit path that continued on in a straight line beyond the building. This continuation of the path, however, occurred only in the spirit world.

Shamanic landscapes
The feeling of flying in a straight line across the landscape is common to the shamans of many different traditional

> **Ancient peoples believed in the reality of spirit flight, which has left its imprint as various forms of straight lines on what might be described as shamanic landscapes around the world.**

cultures around the world. It may be a function of the human brain in a trance state, brought on by drumming, dancing, fasting, or hallucinatory drugs. But even if shamanic flight is a hallucinatory effect, ancient peoples believed in its reality. It seems likely that this belief has left its imprint as various forms of straight lines on what might be described as shamanic landscapes around the world.

The sound of flight
This painted wooden rattle in the shape of a bird, from Vancouver, Canada, may have been used by a shaman to assist him on his imagined flight.

THE GREAT VISION

At an early age, the Oglala Sioux shaman Black Elk had a great vision in which he flew out of his body and journeyed to the world of the spirits, where he was shown the future.

TRAVELING TOWARD THE ROCKY MOUNTAINS in the summer of 1872, the Oglala Sioux tribe camped one evening beside a creek. While they were eating, a nine-year-old member of the tribe, Black Elk, heard a voice saying "It is time. They are calling you." The boy suddenly went into a coma and remained unconscious for 12 days. He said later that he felt himself move out of his body and had a vision.

Black Elk saw two men come down from the clouds bearing spears. The men took his spirit body with them to the clouds, where he was greeted with formations of horses at each of the four quarters — north, south, east, and west — and by the Grandfathers, who represented the Powers of the World. The Grandfathers took him to the center of the world, showed him the universe, and gave him the power to heal and the power to destroy. They also showed him the sacred hoop of his people, which represented their spiritual unity.

Becoming a shaman

Black Elk was then shown his people starving and in distress, their sacred hoop broken. A voice told him that he had been given the sacred stick, which he should place in the center of the hoop and make it bloom into a tree — the world tree. At the end of his vision, he stood on a high mountain, which he later identified as Harney Mountain in the Black Hills, South Dakota, and saw the sacred hoop mended, and many sacred hoops joined together, with one special tree sheltering all peoples.

When he returned to consciousness, he told no one about what he had seen. When he was 18, he began

reenacting parts of his vision and became a shaman and healer. While having a vision he felt as though he were lifted out of himself and flying through the air.

During his lifetime, Black Elk witnessed the gradual loss of American Indian traditions as Europeans settled the West and the Indians were moved to reservations.

In 1886, he joined Buffalo Bill's Wild West show. He believed that if he understood more about the world of the white man, he could fulfill his vision and help his people. When he returned in 1889, Black Elk found that many of his people were involved in a

> **While having a vision he felt as though he were lifted out of himself and flying through the air.**

movement that prophesied the end of the white race and the restoration of traditional Indian ways. Believing this to fit his vision, he became a follower. The movement ended with the massacre at Wounded Knee creek in 1890. The survivors were dispersed to reservations.

In 1930, Black Elk was interviewed at length by John Neihardt, the American writer who published his recollections in the book *Black Elk Speaks* (1932). According to Neihardt, the shaman's memories provided an insight into the meaning of life as it was for the Indians of the western plains, and as it might be for all people. With the renewal of American Indian interest in traditional ways, Black Elk's vision has partially been fulfilled.

The plea on Harney Mountain
In 1931, Black Elk stood on Harney Mountain, raised his arms and shouted to the empty sky: "O make my people live."

GHOST ROADS

Ancient straight road systems and puzzling alignments of sacred sites may have a simple explanation. Recent research in northern Europe suggests that they may be connected with Viking burial rites.

HREE CURIOUS MINOR ROADS cross heathland between the towns of Laren and Hilversum outside Amsterdam. These roads are perfectly straight and converge on St. John's cemetery. These roads were *Doodwegen*, which means "death roads," medieval tracks used for taking corpses to burial. Long forgotten, they were rediscovered by the British artist John Palmer, who has found death roads at other sites in Holland as well. The local people of De Lutte, in

---

The roots of the tradition of death roads may lie in the Viking practice of carrying a dead chieftain to burial along a special, straight, ritual road.

Twente, Holland, refer to a road that runs through the town as a *dodenweg* ("death road"), *lykweg* ("corpse road"), or *spokenweg* ("spook" or "ghost road").

In the Netherlands a medieval oath had to be sworn at a traditional twice-annual ecclesiastical court by those people who had been charged with transporting the corpse during funerals. The oath reads: "Our corpse-roads are in good order, and we have followed the straight corpse road with the body."

A European tradition

But these medieval death roads are not unique to the Netherlands. They were once found throughout many parts of northern Europe. Earth mysteries researchers are also discovering traces of the death roads in folklore, place names, and ancient archeological sites in Germany, Scandinavia, and Britain.

The roots of the tradition of death roads may lie, some researchers now feel, in the Viking practice of carrying a dead chieftain to burial along a special, straight, ritual road. At Rösaring in Sweden, for instance, archeologists have unearthed a 9th-century Viking road that runs straight to a group of Bronze Age and Iron Age cairns (burial mounds constructed from piles of boulders) at its southern end. The chieftain's body was placed in a death house at the northern end of the road, and after a ceremony was held, the body

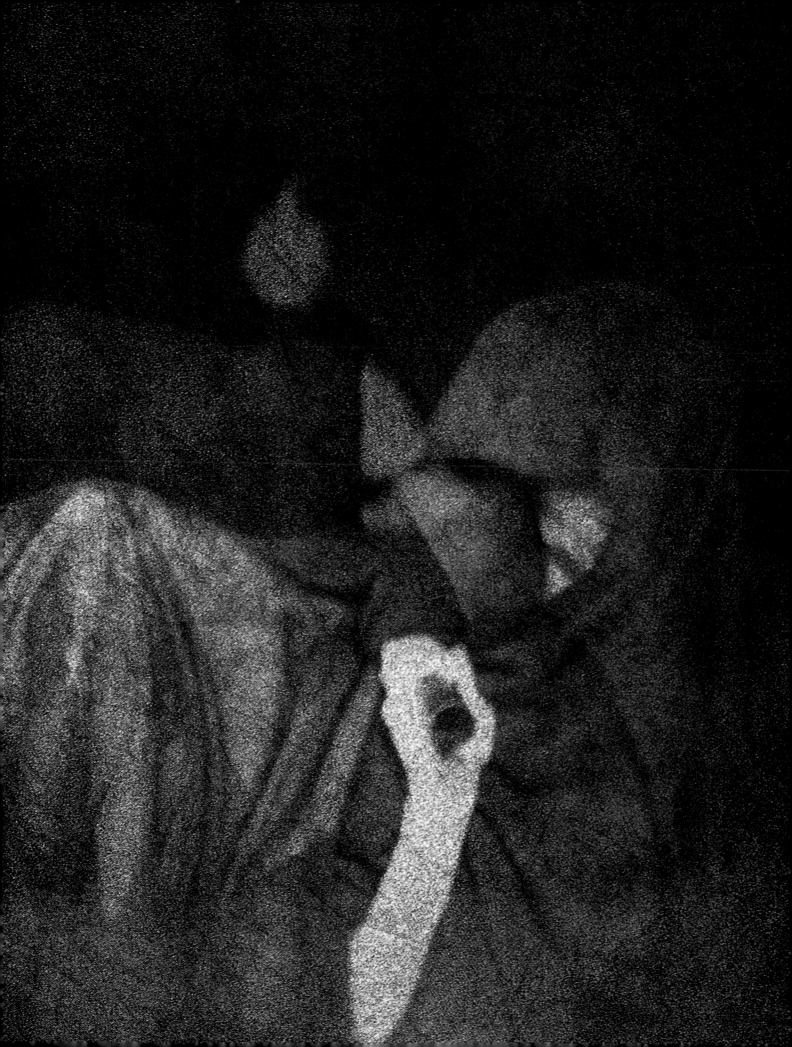

was drawn along the straight road in a large ceremonial wagon to its final resting place among the cairns.

German ghost paths

Geisterwege, which means "ghost paths," were also found in parts of Germany. The *Handworterbuch des deutschen Aberglaubens* ("*Handbook of German Superstitions*," 1933) contains this entry: "Ghost paths are always in the same place, and on them one often meets with ghosts. The paths, without exception, always run in a straight line over mountains and valleys and through marshes. In the towns, they pass the houses close by or sometimes even go right through them. The paths always end or originate at a cemetery. This idea may stem from the ancient custom of driving a corpse along a

> "A dead man's road was believed to have the same characteristics as a cemetery; it is a place where spirits of the deceased thrive."
>
> **Handbook of German Superstitions**

Viking burial mound
This impressive mound in the forest was built by the Vikings to hold the body of one of their chieftains. The Vikings also placed their dead leaders in ships for their final journey. This mound is near the Oseberg burial ship on the Oslo Fjord in Norway.

special dead man's road. This road was believed to have the same characteristics as a cemetery; it is a place where spirits of the deceased thrive."

The ley connection

These ancient German customs were recorded in the 19th century. It was only later, in 1921, that Alfred Watkins discovered in Britain the alignments of

ancient sites that he called leys. Despite being apparently unrelated to them, ghost paths bear a striking similarity to Watkins's description of leys.

Some ley researchers now suspect that the alignments they have been finding in the British countryside may be remnants of medieval death roads, associated with ancient burial practices. They speculate that the ancient sites, churches, and such natural landmarks as springs, hills, or ancient fords that often occur along the leys are, in some cases, merely chance alignments. One example of a ley that might have been a ghost path passes through the large, prehistoric earthworked hill called Sutton Walls, just north of Hereford in England. Watkins described this line in his book *The Old Straight Track* (1925). From a gap on the distant horizon between the main earthworks of Sutton Walls and a small mound, Watkins saw the spire of Marden church and the tower of Wellington church a few miles away in alignment. The line then passed through the gap and on through the cemetery at Sutton St. Nicholas church. It ended at Weston Beggard church.

In 1924, a year after Alfred Watkins discovered this alignment, a farmer told him that when he plowed the field at the foot of Sutton Walls, he made out the dark line of an old straight track leading to the gap. Watkins believed that it, too, fell on the alignment he had found.

British corpse ways

Many British folk tales refer to "corpse ways." According to tradition, a funeral party traveling on foot created a right-of-way wherever it went. These rights-of-way may have been the original corpse ways.

More research is needed to establish whether these corpse ways were indeed actual tracks along which the funeral party carried the corpse. If this could be established, then the tracks might share a common origin with the Dutch death roads and the German ghost paths.

AVENUES OF THE DEAD

Once believed to be Roman racetracks, the large British landscape features known as cursuses may be Neolithic ley lines, religious centers, or connected with ancient burial rites.

LOOKING WEST along a segment of the Dorset cursus toward a burial mound with which it is aligned, archeologist Richard Bradley, of Reading University, England, watched the dying midwinter sun sink into the ancient mound. This chance sighting caused Bradley to conclude that the cursus "links the positions of the ancestors with the movement of the heavenly bodies." Bradley refers to the cursus as "a British Avenue of the Dead."

In addition the cursus is linked to nearby burial mounds not just by solar alignments but also in a more physical way. Excavations reveal that mounds near the cursus were connected to it by straight avenues of poles.

Structure of a cursus

Bradley's opinions on the function of the Dorset cursus combine guesswork with archeological evidence. Yet while no one can be sure what cursuses were actually used for, the structure of these mysterious landmarks is well understood.

Cursuses are long, narrow enclosures bounded by banks and external ditches. Typically about 300 feet wide, they can be up to several miles in length. Most cursuses are straight, and many point to a river.

Because they usually connect prehistoric burial mounds and are often found near henges (circular or oval formations of standing stones), it is suspected that the cursuses may have been used for religious rituals.

Ley researcher Paul Devereux studied about half of Britain's cursuses, most of which are so eroded that they are now visible only from the air. Nonetheless, he found that 64 percent point to either a prehistoric site or an ancient church (which he assumes stood on an even earlier sacred site).

Cemetery stone
This church at Rudston was built beside the largest standing stone in England; one of three cursuses near the village aligns to it.

THE STONEHENGE CURSUS

In 1947 archeologist J. F. S. Stone noticed that if he extended the line of the northern ditch almost a mile beyond the eastern end of the Stonehenge cursus, it would pass through a standing stone remnant known as the Cuckoo Stone and a Neolithic ritual site named Woodhenge. Extending this line some miles farther leads to a ridge called Beacon Hill.

This alignment of ancient sites has all the features of a ley line as defined by Alfred Watkins. In *Lines on the Landscape* (1989), Paul Devereux and Nigel Pennick linked leys and cursuses: "We have here remains which tell us that Neolithic people did make linear links between some of their sites. Even if this cursus ley [at Stonehenge] were the only evidence available, Watkins's basic contention is vindicated."

What's in a name?
Antiquarian William Stukeley discovered the Stonehenge cursus in 1723. He called it a cursus, *the Latin for "racetrack," since he believed that this was its purpose in Roman times. The name is now used for all such sites.*

MYSTERY LINES OF THE AMERICAS

Some ancient peoples incised long straight lines or drew elaborate figures in the earth. The most striking and mysterious examples are found in the Americas.

*M*ILES FROM ANYWHERE, in the midst of the barren landscape of the Peruvian pampas, a woman stood carefully sweeping clear the faint lines that had been drawn in the desert by a mysterious people more than 1,000 years earlier. The bright yellow subsoil that she uncovered stood out in contrast to the dark rocky desert. The woman stopped frequently to measure and draw what she had found, for the lines stretched hundreds of feet in each direction, making it impossible to see the whole pattern from the ground.

Maria Reiche uncovered enormous animal figures such as spiders and hummingbirds.

She had already uncovered enormous animal figures such as spiders and hummingbirds. As she followed a huge spiral, sweeping and drawing the image on paper, she wondered what it might be. When at last it was revealed as the tail of a monkey, she laughed aloud.

The woman was Maria Reiche. A German citizen, Reiche trained as a mathematician, but moved to Peru in 1932 and worked as a teacher and translator. Ten years later, she began working on the lines.

The lines in Peru that Maria Reiche swept clear with her broom are by no means unique either in the Americas or in the world. Ancient peoples have often used the earth as a sketchbook. In the Americas, straight linear markings were made by many Indian cultures, among them the Anasazi, the Incas, and the Nazcas.

The Nazca lines

Archeologists believe that the lines in the Peruvian desert were made by the Nazca people between about 100 B.C. and A.D. 700. They cover

A Nazca jar
The bold outlines of people and animals in this design are similar to the figures in the desert.

124

ONE CONTINUOUS LINE

Almost all of the dozens of animal figures on the Nazca plain are drawn in continuous lines, thus making it possible to walk along each figure as though it were a maze. There are, in fact, depressions in the soil that run down the center of these lines that might have been made by the feet of the ancient Nazca people as they followed the lines.

Since the outlines of the animal figures and the hundreds of spirals that grace the desert clearly lead nowhere, they were not ordinary paths. Modern scholars suspect that there was a religious reason for walking the lines. Just as mazes and labyrinths found in medieval European churches were walked to aid concentration and prayer, so the Nazca lines may have had a similar function for the people who created them.

Pathways to spirit flight?

The feeling of disorientation experienced by researcher Evan Hadingham as he traced one of these figures on foot hints at a shamanic use for the lines. Ancient peoples used a variety of methods such as drugs, fasting, or even dancing to bring them closer to the world of the spirits and to produce the sensation of flight. The Nazca shamans may have walked the continuous line figures of the pampa in order to induce the trance state necessary to experience "magical flight."

Desert spider
This 150-foot-long spider was the first of the drawings that Maria Reiche uncovered at Nazca.

BOLIVIAN TRACKS

On the high plain, or *altiplano,* of western Bolivia, many old straight Indian tracks can be found — some of them up to 20 miles long — even longer than any of the lines found at Nazca.

The French anthropologist Alfred Métraux explored them in the early 1930's. He found shrines set out in straight rows leading from a small village on the altiplano. These rows stretched for several miles and were placed along paths that were "absolutely straight, regardless of the irregularities in the ground."

The examples Métraux studied did not seem to have been in use. The local Aymara Indians offered no explanation for them. Either they did not know anything about the lines or they were unwilling to give away their secrets.

Fading lines

During the 1960's, British researcher Tony Morrison visited the area to search for some of the lines on the ground. He found that the lines were fading into the landscape as brush grew over them. In some places, however, it seemed that the older inhabitants of the altiplano were maintaining the lines.

Some of the pagan holy places on these old straight paths have been Christianized with adobe shrines or even churches being built on the sites. In 1985, American anthropologist Johan Reinhard witnessed an Indian procession along one of the lines that led to a mountaintop. Dancing and making music, the Indians walked the line to and from the peak, where they made offerings to a local deity, appealing for water.

Desert sketchbook
Most of the Nazca lines are not animals or spirals but long, straight lines or geometric figures. They cover the pampa as far as the eye can see.

a vast area of about 150 square miles on the desert tablelands, or pampas, between the towns of Nazca and Palpa in the northern part of Peru.

The Nazca people lived in the coastal area of Peru before the time of the Incas. Little is known of them: they left behind only shards of pottery and mysterious lines drawn across the desert.

The lines were made by removing stones and soil on the desert's surface to reveal a lighter, yellow sand beneath. The desert rocks turn a dark brown as their surfaces slowly decompose and oxides are deposited on top of them. This coloration is called desert varnish.

There are three types of Nazca lines: straight lines up to five miles long that crisscross the pampas; realistic line drawings of animals; and some that were not lines at all but huge geometric forms, often trapezoids and triangles.

Unraveling the mystery

Over the years, many researchers have attempted to unravel the mystery of the lines. The most bizarre theory was put forward by bestselling author Erich von Däniken, who claimed that they were built as landing strips for interplanetary spacecraft in some unspecified prehistoric period. Serious researchers reject von Däniken's unsubstantiated theories about ancient astronauts. But many have struggled to answer the core

question: "Why did a people who could not fly draw patterns on the landscape that could be appreciated in their entirety only from the air?"

Seeing the whole picture

The Peruvian archeologist Toribio Mejia Xesspe, one of the first archeologists to record the lines, responded by suggesting that they were ceremonial roads, much like the Inca *ceques.* His account of the lines drew other scholars. Paul Kosok, of Long Island University, arrived in 1941 and watched in awe as the midwinter solstice sun set directly over the end of one of the lines. Kosok concluded that the mysterious lines were "the largest

---

"Why did a people who could not fly draw patterns on the desert that could be appreciated in their entirety only from the air?"

---

astronomy book in the world." Maria Reiche, who studied the Nazca lines longer than anyone else, also believed that they have astronomical significance. Other scholars now believe, however, that the huge lines were not laid out as astronomical sightlines. Gerald Hawkins,

wheel. At least one line from such a center connects with another center. The positioning of the lines seems to have related to water in various ways — they are often found at the river valley edges of the pampas, over ancient subterranean canals, or alongside the numerous fossilized riverbeds (known as *quebradas* in Spanish) on the pampa.

A Nazca maze

Aveni's team also discovered well-worn trails, now covered by desert varnish and visible only as sunken paths, within some of the straight line patterns. But despite the presence of these trails, the Nazca markings are not ordinary tracks or roads, since they neither start nor end at any obviously significant place. It seems possible that some of the lines were used for ritual walking. The animal figures are all drawn in a continuous line, so they can be walked much like a maze.

Some archeologists believe that certain lines may have been pilgrimage paths associated with Cahuachi, a major Nazcan religious center just south of the pampa. Helaine Silverman, of the University of Illinois, believes that "the Nazca priest-scientists observed the natural and supernatural world from Cahuachi and from the pampa."

Keeping the lines open

Silverman and American anthropologist Gary Urton also suspect that the lines, during their period of use, were ritually swept and cleaned. Different lines would doubtless have been the responsibility of various kinship groups, as were the ceques at Cuzco. Ritual sweeping is still practiced, now as part of Catholic religious ceremony, in some Andean villages. A relic of

Inca roads
As well as the mysterious ceques that radiated out from the Temple of the Sun, the Coricancha, *in Cuzco, Peru, the Incas also had a well-developed road system. This is a typical wide Inca road, running straight across the Peruvian desert.*

who had previously written about the astronomical significance of Stonehenge, surveyed the lines in the 1960's and fed data about the lines and the movements of the heavenly bodies into a computer. According to his findings, there seemed to be no statistically significant astronomical rationale for the lines.

New studies, conducted in the 1980's by a team led by Dr. Anthony F. Aveni of Colgate University in Hamilton, New York, found that some lines might have marked sunrise or sunset at the summer and winter solstices. But there are so many lines scattered across the desert, lines probably executed over hundreds of years, that it would be strange if some of them did not form alignments with astronomical events.

The ray centers

Dr. Aveni and his colleagues also studied over 60 network patterns, which other researchers call ray centers, embedded in the mesh of straight lines. Maria Reiche had already charted many of these patterns. The lines radiate from the ray centers — central points, such as hills or mounds topped with piles of boulders — like spokes from the hub of a

Lady of the lines
From 1946, Maria Reiche lived in the desert, charting the lines. She spent nearly 50 years of her life in an attempt to unravel their mystery.

pre-Columbian religion, this modern ritual may be rooted in the ancient past, suggesting that the Nazca lines were also ritually swept by ancient peoples.

It is known that the Nazca people had a complex society that existed before the time of the Incas. Shards of Nazca pottery provide archeologists with clues to the dates of the desert drawings as well as to the people who made them. In certain areas — particularly in the north, where most of the animal figures are clustered — pottery has been found on the surface of the desert. It dates from the height of Nazca culture, about 100 B.C. to A.D. 100. Archeologists believe the pots were left as offerings to the gods.

Searching for clues
Elsewhere on the pampa, another, cruder type of ceramic has been found. These shards were probably from water jars. Canadian archeologist Persis B. Clarkson surveyed hundreds of miles of the pampa on foot, examining the lines for man-made objects, such as pottery and cairns. The few shards she found were clustered around the ray centers. The purpose and history of the Nazca lines that has emerged from the most recent scholarly research is complicated. Dr. Aveni sums it up: "Our overall conclusions point toward a broad range of explanations for the lines, not any single theory." He believes that the key to the lines lies in a complex combination of the following factors: "Water, walking, astronomy, kinship, division of labor and ceremonial responsibility, sweeping, [and] radiality."

The Chaco roads
In the semiarid high mesa country of northwest New Mexico, researchers are still trying to explain the presence and function of a remarkable network of roads that radiates in straight lines for many miles around Chaco Canyon. Unlike trails that follow the contours of the landscape, these roads, which were a standard 30 feet wide, were deliberately engineered. The surfaces of the roads were either made of compacted earth or cut into the bedrock. Staircases up to 25 feet wide were carved out of the rock of the canyon sides as part of this road network. Most of the roads are absolutely straight. One runs north: over its entire 45-mile length it varies by only a few degrees from true north.

These roads were made by an ancient American Indian farming people called the Anasazi, who emerged around 300 B.C. and gradually developed their

Making tracks
The Chaco roads run in straight lines across the landscape and measure a standard 30 feet across. But most have faded into the landscape and are no longer visible on the ground. This photograph dates from 1916 and shows a horse-drawn carriage on a Chaco road near Aztec, New Mexico.

Pueblo Bonito
In the region around Chaco Canyon, 150 Great Houses, or pueblos, have been found, including 9 within the canyon itself. They were connected by an elaborate network of roads. The magnificent complex of Pueblo Bonito, built in the 11th century A.D., was the heart of the Anasazi settlement in the canyon.

MAYAN HIGHWAYS

The Mayas of the Yucatán Peninsula of southeastern Mexico built a network of roads to connect their cities from A.D. 300. These straight roads are called *sacbeob*. Only fragments of the road network survive, and some may still await discovery within the dense rain forests of Central America.

The longest-known sacbeob links Coba with Yaxuna 62 miles away in the north of the Yucatán, not far from Chichén Itzá. In the 1920's the explorer Thomas Gann described the road as: "a great elevated road or causeway 32 feet wide....This was one of the most remarkable roads ever constructed, as the sides were built of great blocks of cut stone, many weighing hundreds of pounds." He marveled that it was "straight as an arrow, and almost flat as a rule."

Segments of sacbeob link the settlements on the island of Cozumel, a place of Mayan pilgrimage off the peninsula's northeast coast. Scientists have mapped over three miles of the best-preserved section that runs between San Gervasio and the island's northeast coast. They believe it was five feet wide, with shrines posted along it.

Chichén Itzá
This Mayan city, which was founded in about the 6th century A.D., is linked to other cities in the Yucatán by a network of roads, known as sacbeobs. One of the city's major monuments, the Castillo, or great pyramid, is in the background.

Mayan figurine
This terra-cotta funerary sculpture of a woman writing was found in a tomb on the island of Jaina off the Yucatán Peninsula, Mexico.

distinctive style of flat-roofed buildings made of mud, rock, and posts, which are known as pueblos. Chaco Canyon was their cultural hub. The pueblos they built there grew over the years into large multi-storied and terraced complexes or Great Houses, with walls, courtyards, and *kivas*, ceremonial chambers whose function can only be guessed at.

The roads the Anasazi left behind have faded into the landscape and are now often difficult to see at ground level. Archeologists have mapped some 400 miles of the Chaco roads, using aerial photography combined with ground surveys and excavation. The roads lead to 80 villages within a 100-mile radius of the Chaco canyon, changing direction only occasionally, usually at a natural landmark or Great House.

To the modern observer, there seems to be no obvious practical reason for the Anasazi, who had neither the horse (which was introduced to the Americas by the Spaniards) or the wheel, to have built such elaborate roads. Foot travel does not require such complex roads.

Many researchers now believe that these roads were ceremonial or sacred ways linking the Great Houses, which may have been centers for ritual.

Appeasing the spirits

Fragments of pottery vessels have been discovered in patches along some of the Chaco roads, especially in areas close to Great Houses. Some archeologists say that the pots were broken during trading expeditions, while others believe they were smashed during religious rituals. In many southwestern cultures, pottery vessels were broken to appease spirits, particularly those of the dead.

But although we know more than ever before about these roads, their function still remains a mystery. NASA scientist Thomas L. Sever was involved with a project that revealed through infrared photographs that the roads had multiple parallel sections. Sever warns: "we must not transfer our concept of modern-day roads into the prehistoric past." But the ancient road builders seem to have taken their secrets with them to the grave.

> NASA scientist Thomas L. Sever warns: "We must not transfer our concept of modern-day roads into the prehistoric past."

RULER LINES

European palaces were monuments to absolutist government — the scale of the buildings, and the design of the road systems around them, were graphic proof of the monarch's authority over his subjects.

AROUND THE WORLD governments build imposing edifices approached by magnificent avenues to house their offices. At this central point, decisions are made and orders are sent out. This modern image of a seat of government is rooted in concepts of kingship that originated in Renaissance Europe.

Nexus of power

The rulers of Renaissance Europe, secure on their thrones, no longer needed castles defended by massive walls, moats, and earthworks to protect them from invading armies. Instead they wanted to impress their subjects with their power. To this end, they ordered beautifully designed complexes of palaces, parks, and cities to be built. From the palace,

St. Peter's
The road leading up to Saint Peter's Basilica in Vatican City, Rome, ends in a piazza surrounded by a colonnade which was designed by Gian Lorenzo Bernini in 1656. Its grandeur reflects the power of the Roman Catholic Church.

Buckingham Palace
This palace in central London was originally built by the dukes of Buckingham but has been used by the British royal family as a residence since 1761. A broad, imposing avenue called The Mall leads to the palace, forming a route for ceremonial processions.

Capitals built in the 20th century in India and Australia continue the Old World tradition of trying to impose order on the landscape.

unbroken straight roads radiated out across the country as far as the eye could see, symbolizing the king's power extending throughout the land.

Similarly imposing designs were adopted even in countries that rejected the notion of absolute rule by a king or queen. The layout of Washington, D.C., designed by Pierre Charles L'Enfant in 1791, followed the European model.

Capitals built in the 20th century, such as New Delhi, India, and Canberra, Australia, continue the Old World tradition of trying to impose order on the landscape by the symbolic use of architecture.

Versailles
The vast scale of the palace built for the French king Louis XIV at Versailles in the 17th century was intended to reflect his absolute power over the whole country.

A GERMAN PALACE

Built in 1715 for Karl Wilhelm, Duke of Baden, the city of Karlsruhe is laid out according to plans for holy cities described in ancient German mystical writings.

At the center of the city is the duke's palace, from which 32 evenly spaced roads radiate out into the surrounding area. Some run through the forest to the north, while others make up the streets of the city to the south. These straight roads link the palace to important features in the landscape, including churches, a mausoleum, and the royal palace at Mannheim.

A south-facing seat

The main axis of Karlsruhe runs south from the palace along the main street. It was traditional in northern Europe during the early middle ages for the lord to sit in

The White House
The president's residence in Washington, D.C., was designed as an integral part of the city. Washington has a symmetrical, double-axis layout. Eight diagonal streets radiate from the seat of Congress, the Capitol Building.

The Raj Path
In New Delhi, India, the British architect Edwin Lutyens designed a new seat of government in 1911. It features a major east-west axis, Central Vista Park, with Government House as its focal point. The road known as the Raj Path runs through the park, leading from the presidential palace to a memorial arch.

The palace and park at Karlsruhe in Germany

the north, which was believed to be the place of the gods. Like these early Germanic kings, Karl Wilhelm faced south. The Swabian Alps are visible on the horizon 45 miles due south, directly opposite the palace itself.

Imposing architectural features were placed along the main street of Karlsruhe. These include a pyramid in the middle of the main square, monuments and obelisks along the way, and a church atop a hill at the end of the road.

Sans Souci Palace
This palace in Potsdam, Germany, was built between 1744 and 1752. It was designed on a grand scale, with roads and paths symbolizing lines of power radiating out into the surrounding countryside.

CHAPTER SIX

FOREVER SACRED

Throughout the world the monuments of ancient peoples and the sites they regarded as sacred are being destroyed by the practices of modern society. Many people believe it is time to review our treatment of these places, and prevent any further interference before they are lost forever.

At the beginning of the world, according to the creation myth of the Hopi Indians, a rhythmic sound caused life to spring forth in every corner of the globe. But this creative energy did not spread itself evenly. At some places, the Hopi believe, it was more concentrated than at others. They call these places "the spots on the fawn" and believe that they are especially powerful and therefore sacred. For they allow human beings to make closer contact with the

spiritual world and are used by the Hopi in their religious and ceremonial activities.

Of course, the Hopi are not alone in believing that some areas are more sacred than others. There seems to be a deep-seated need in the human psyche to mark out certain places as sacred. Romanian-born anthropologist Mircea Eliade has said, "Men are not free to choose the sacred site...they only find it by the help of mysterious signs."

Such signs vary from culture to culture. For some people, such as the American Indians, the presence of certain animals may indicate a place of power, since they are believed to be more closely attuned to the ways of the earth. In other parts of the world, geological anomalies such as ringing rocks, strange lights and noises, and increased magnetism occur at sacred places. Such phenomena may have been the reason that people first considered these places to be sacred. Mountains, rivers, lakes, strange rocks, and waterfalls are often thought to be sacred as well.

Human influences

The mysterious powers believed to exist at a site may be either enhanced or hampered by the actions of humans. In some cultures structures such as temples or shrines like Delphi, and monuments like Stonehenge and the Pyramids, were probably built on sites believed to possess strange powers, and people were encouraged to visit them.

Sometimes figures were drawn on the ground or on rocks. Other cultures left sacred sites in their natural state. This is true of most American Indian tribes, as well as the Australian Aborigines. Most Indian tribes teach that visitors to sacred sites must undergo certain rituals to purify themselves and to prepare them for their encounter with the sacred. Failing to perform these time-honored rituals correctly, they believe, is potentially dangerous both for the visitor, who could be harmed by the powers at the site, and for the sacred place itself, whose mysterious powers could be diminished if they were misused.

Sacred sites in the modern world

Today many sacred sites are visited, often by tourists, either because they have played an important role in world history or culture or because of their outstanding natural or architectural beauty. A few are still used for religious purposes.

Intense controversy has erupted in some areas over the use of such lands for mining and other commercial purposes.

> **There seems to be a deep-seated need in the human psyche to mark out certain places as sacred.**

Smokescreen
The huge columns of smoke discharged from an industrial site in Gallup, New Mexico, diffuse into the surrounding landscape, which is a reservation for the Navajos.

The Four Corners area, where Arizona, Utah, New Mexico, and Colorado meet, is rich in coal, uranium, and gold. It is also sacred to the Navajos and Hopis who think that the nearby mountains are home to rain spirits, known as *kachinas*, and that the entire landscape is sacred and should not be desecrated by outsiders.

The south-western desert land has been baked a deep, warm red by the sun, and rugged rock formations and mountains stand out against the skies. But amidst this natural splendor, the land has been scarred by strip mines gouging coal from the ground, fouled by emissions from the Four Corners power station which now dominates the arid landscape, and threatened by pollution from uranium mines.

National sacrifice areas

Much of this land is Indian land. The National Academy of Sciences has called places throughout America where strip mining occurs "national sacrifice areas" because of the damage the mining does to the environment. Some people believe that the Indians who live nearby have already sacrificed too much and should not have to sacrifice their land as well.

Some Indians now want to restrict the commercial use of their lands in order to preserve their culture and sacred sites. But the ever-increasing demands of the rest of the country for energy make the exploitation of the mineral reserves

Staying put
Navajo and Hopi people have shared reservation land in Arizona since 1882. Relocation was proposed, but most refuse to leave an area that they believe to be sacred. A few, like this Navajo woman, threatened to fight for their land.

desirable. Conflict between these two points of view occurs around the world. In Australia the Aborigines are demanding the right to decide what happens to their lands. In the Amazon rain forests of Brazil the native people are trying to stop their way of life from being destroyed along with the forests, which are being cleared by loggers and farmers at a rate of thousands of square miles per day.

Conservationists argue that to save the planet we must change the way we live on it. They say that we should listen to native peoples, such as the Kogi Indians of Colombia, who ask that the people of the industrialized world change their ways before they destroy the planet. The Kogis reject any outside influences, such as cars, electricity, and even shoes, that they believe may threaten their traditional way of life.

Many places under threat from mining, logging, or other forms of development are considered sacred.

Remembering the dead
American Indians visited Wounded Knee, South Dakota, to commemorate the centennial of the massacre of hundreds of Sioux on December 20, 1890. The grave at the site where victims of the massacre are buried is sacred to their memory.

FREE TO BELIEVE
In 1978 Congress passed the American Indian Religious Freedom Act, which specifically addressed the issue of access to sacred sites, stating that "laws and policies often deny American Indians access to sacred sites required in their religion, including cemeteries." It sought to redress this by requiring that it become "the policy of the United States to protect and preserve for American Indians their inherent right of freedom to believe, express, and exercise the religions of the American Indian, Eskimo, Aleut, and native Hawaiians, including access to sites...."

Lobbying for change
American Indians set up camp outside the White House to press for legal recognition of their right to religious freedom in 1978.

135

Members of American Indian religions believe that to remain holy, these places must remain unspoiled.

The Navajo believe that the San Francisco Peaks in Arizona, which they call *Doo-ko-oslid*, are sacred, but the

Returning the land
On October 26, 1985, the Australian government formally handed ownership of Ayers Rock back to the Aborigines, for whom it has always been a sacred site.

United States Forest Service allowed new skiing areas on the mountain in the Coconino National Forest to be built. The Navajo Tribal Council objected, warning that if this development occurred, "The rain and snow will cease to fall; the Navajo people will be unprotected from the forces of destruction; our traditions will die, and Doo-ko-oslid will turn away from us."

Protecting the sacred

The Australian government is committed to land rights: the policy of giving vacant land owned by the government back to the Aborigines if they can prove a hereditary connection to the area. This policy has resulted in the transfer of Ayers Rock,

Australia's most famous sacred site, to the Aborigines, who now manage the site and allow visitors to view it. To protect the site, which they call Uluru, tourists are no longer allowed to climb the rock.

Center of conflict

Coronation Hill, a low hill in Australia's Northern Territory, became the focus of the kind of dispute that occurs whenever minerals are found in a place considered to be sacred. About $500 million worth of gold, platinum, and palladium are thought to lie beneath Coronation Hill. These minerals will remain there undisturbed, however, because after many years of debate and study, the government concluded that the site is sacred to the Aboriginal Jawoyn tribe. According to John Ah Kit, a Jawoyn leader, "The Jawoyn believe that if the mining goes ahead, Bula [a spirit who

> ## The minerals will remain undisturbed because the site is sacred to the Aboriginal Jawoyn tribe.

roamed Australia during the Dreamtime, the mythical time when the land was believed to have been created] will physically shake the country, and there will be an apocalyptic calamity — tidal waves and earthquakes. There will be no sun and moon — only wind and rain, and everything will be destroyed...."

The perils of war
An international effort has been launched to restore Cambodia's most sacred site, the Angkor temple, which has been damaged by war and weather. During restoration, the temple is constantly guarded to discourage looters.

◆ PAGE 138

TRAMPLING HISTORY UNDERFOOT

With the rise of tourism in the modern age, the number of people visiting the world's most famous and mysterious sites has risen to the point where they have begun to cause irreparable damage.

MASS TOURISM IS A MODERN PHENOMENON: Before the Second World War only a million people traveled abroad each year, but by the year 2000 experts estimate that 650 million people will do so. These large numbers are capable of doing serious damage. Greece has suffered more than most tourist destinations, and the Greek Orthodox Church even has a prayer for deliverance from tourists: "Lord Jesus, have mercy on the cities, the islands and the villages of this Orthodox Fatherland ...scourged by the worldly touristic wave."

A delicate beauty

Clearly, tourism is a two-edged sword, for while crowds of visitors can do great harm to some sites, they also bring money that can help preserve them. This financial boon has done a great deal to preserve Africa's wildlife — for instance, the 5,500 people who visit Rwanda each year to see the gorillas bring in $500,000, thereby making the animals a valuable part of the country's economy, and giving the government an incentive to take action against poachers.

Chaco Canyon
The desolate bulk of the Fajada Butte in the right background is the site of the Anasazi Sun Dagger, an ancient sundial that works as a calendar. The site has been so severely eroded by tourists' hiking boots that its alignments no longer work. The Park Service has closed it to the public.

But in many places the sheer numbers of visitors can cause problems. At Nôtre Dame in Paris, for example, 108 people walk through the doors every minute. And the tourist buses waiting outside emit fumes that damage the stonework of the cathedral.

Ancient sacred sites are particularly vulnerable. The ground around the standing stones at Carnac in Brittany, for instance, has been so badly eroded by visitors' boots that the stones are in danger of falling over. A major part of the site was closed to the public in 1991, for seven years, so that the earth around the stones could be restored and new pathways could be constructed to keep visitors away from the stones. Visitors must now view many of the stones from a special platform. Stonehenge, too, has been roped off so that visitors cannot enter the circle or touch the stones. In addition, since controlling the visitors is a problem, access is denied at sunrise and sunset on the summer solstice, normally the most popular time for Stonehenge enthusiasts.

Vulgar vandals

Stonehenge and Carnac have been damaged inadvertently by sheer force of numbers, but vandalism has also occurred. Graffiti has been scribbled on ancient stones since Roman times, but with more visitors the problem has increased.

Some of the worst damage has been caused by vehicles driving across the markings on the desert floor at Nazca in Peru and near Blythe, California. With little wind and almost no rain to erase them, drawings and other marks remain on the desert floor for hundreds of years: the tire tracks will be there just as long — perhaps puzzling future archeologists and certainly spoiling the beauty of the lines for future generations.

According to some anthropologists, tourism is a kind of secular pilgrimage. People leave their daily lives and turn to places of great natural beauty or spiritual significance to find something that they lack — perhaps it is a sense of the sacred. But in searching for it, they often damage the very thing that they were looking for.

A LIVING LEGACY

The international community has banded together to protect sites of special interest around the world. In 1972 the United Nations Educational, Scientific, and Cultural Organization (UNESCO) drew up a document called the World Heritage Convention to safeguard the earth's cultural and natural heritage. So far the convention has been ratified by 108 nations.

There are 315 sites on the list, many of which are, or once were, sacred places. Among them are: the Cahokia Mounds, Mesa Verde National Park, Chaco Canyon National Historical Park, Stonehenge, Cuzco, Machupicchu, Delphi, the Vatican, and Jerusalem.

Aid for repairs

Through aid packages, UNESCO also helps poorer nations to keep sites of special interest in good repair. Borobudur in Indonesia was one such site. UNESCO funds allowed it to be completely restored in the 1970's. It is now used as a temple again.

However, the tribe was divided as to whether or not the hill was part of Bula's sacred resting place, an area known as Sickness Country. Some said that they welcomed development, since they believed that Coronation Hill was not part of Sickness Country. Anthropologists were called in to give evidence, as were tribal elders. In 1991 the Australian Cabinet settled the matter by refusing to allow mining to procede. The Jawoyn leader who said, "They can offer us millions of dollars, but we will not trade our sacred sites," had won his battle.

Knowledge of the ancients

Hidden in the temples and monuments, carvings, paintings, and even the earthly remains of the people who created these places are clues to their way of life. But these places and the relics that remain in them are a finite resource. They require the active efforts and specialized skills of

archeologists and other scientists if they are to be preserved for generations to come: extremes of weather, and even the very passage of time can cause damage.

The murals at Chichén Itzá in Mexico's Yucatán Peninsula show a way of life that vanished with the Mayas, but now even the spectacular paintings themselves are disappearing. Once the murals were uncovered by explorers, the hot, humid climate and the relentless sun faded the colors, particularly the intense shade known as Maya blue. Parts of the murals have since been chipped away by vandals or taken as souvenirs by tourists. What remains has been attacked by algae. The colors in the murals could help us understand the Maya, for they are of symbolic importance. It is, however, too late to save these vibrant colors. Luckily, they were recorded for posterity by the English watercolorist Adela Catherine Breton, who, from 1900 to 1908, made painstakingly accurate copies of the murals.

Partnership with the past

Such records keep historical data from being lost, even if the originals are later destroyed or damaged, as the Mayan murals were. For this reason, archeologists publish detailed records of their findings, including photographs and drawings of the various stages of excavation. Anthropologists' data on the rituals of American Indians, for example, have been used by their descendants to reconstruct their ancient religions and bring them back to life.

Partnerships between anthropologists and archeologists and the people they are studying help to preserve native cultures, benefiting both groups. In the past, however, the work of archeologists sometimes amounted to little more than robbery and desecration, as goods were taken from tombs and artworks were ripped off walls to furnish museums.

A fragile inheritance

Ancient sites and sacred landscapes are among the wonders of the world. Forests cut down for logging may take hundreds of years to grow back, but cave paintings attacked by bacteria brought in by tourists may never recover, and modern

> ## "They can offer us millions of dollars, but we will not trade our sacred sites."

industrial techniques used to take minerals from the earth may wreak havoc with fragile eco-systems.

The earth's sacred places also allow us a glimpse of other world views and ways of seeing things. They provide a mental and spiritual heritage in addition to the physical one of monuments, shrines, burial mounds, and temples, and the artwork that adorns them. To keep this legacy of consciousness, it is perhaps wiser to err on the side of caution and preserve these sites wherever and whenever possible.

In our modern, rational world it is not generally thought that the landscape can affect the human personality. But in the world of the ancients this idea was accepted. In the fourth century B.C., the Greek philosopher Plato wrote in *The Laws*: "Some localities have a more marked tendency than others to produce better or worse men. Most markedly conspicuous of all will be localities which are the homes of some supernatural influence, or the haunts of spirits who give a gracious or ungracious reception...."

The vanishing spirit of place

But the spirits can be unpredictable. Those at the San Francisco Peaks did not stop the rain and snow from falling when a ski resort was built there, although many Navajo believed they would. Yet while the spirits may not rise against us if we desecrate their sacred places, some fear the greater danger that the spirits may vanish forever along with the sites they once inhabited.

Signature stone
Graffiti is nothing new. In the 18th century, the English poet Lord Byron (1788—1824) carved his name in stone at the Temple of Poseidon in Sounion, Greece.

Art and archeology
This detail of the south wall of the Temple of the Jaguars in Chichén Itzá, painted by Adela Breton, shows a battle scene in all its brilliance; the mural itself has now faded.

WHO OWNS THE PAST?

Archeologists study the material remains of the peoples of the past: the structures they built, the objects they used, and even their bodily remains. But where those people have living descendants, conflict about who owns the past can often arise.

Good practice
Using a dental probe, a researcher delicately cleans a 1,200-year-old Anglo-Saxon skeleton excavated in Yorkshire, England. After recording and examining the bones, the whole skeleton was given a Christian funeral service and reburied on site.

History for sale
Guaqueros ("grave robbers") plunder graves in Colombia for artifacts to sell to collectors, destroying the sites for archeological excavation. They often break the very objects that they wish to sell as they wrench them from the ground.

I N THE 19TH AND EARLY 20TH CENTURIES, great collections of artifacts, from sites all over the world, were amassed by museums and private collectors in Europe and North America. To their former owners, many of these objects had been sacred: Egyptian mummies, South American shrunken heads, and skeletons from Australia.

The 19th-century explorers and archeologists who first excavated ancient sites often destroyed as much material as they uncovered by digging at random in an effort to find buried treasure. The careful methods used by modern archeologists did not become fully accepted until the turn of the century. Today most experts recognize that, "to a certain extent all excavation is destruction." Archeologists now uncover the past with caution; their investigations are often the only source of our knowledge of prehistoric peoples, and they know that once a particular site has been excavated some of its secrets may be lost forever.

A modern scandal

In many countries sites are still routinely plundered by robbers. The objects they find are sold to art collectors. In Guatemala, there are 150 guards to prevent such

pillaging, but they are outnumbered by the grave robbers, so it is impossible to protect the sites. The robbers mine Mayan cities, temples, and graves for treasures that had been safely hidden for more than 1,000 years, and damage the buildings in their search.

Some art dealers claim that the trade in antiquities helps preserve the stolen

Faultless facsimile
This artist is creating a replica of the paintings at Lascaux in France after the originals had to be closed to the public. Although the 25,000-year-old artworks were not discovered until 1940, by the late 1980's, bacteria brought in by the 200,000 annual visitors had produced a mold that had damaged them. The caves are now closed to all but a few scholars. The public, however, can view copies in a cave nearby.

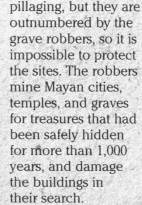

objects since once sold they are kept in good condition. But archeologists decry the trade. In addition to the destruction caused to sites, no records are kept of where the stolen pieces have been discovered. International law, too, prohibits the trade. But the UNESCO convention that outlaws the sale of such cultural treasures has not always been honored by member states. A U.S. law that prohibits the trade in sculptured architectural materials has, however, put a stop to this trade in the States.

Rest in peace

But artifacts are not the only sacred items that have found their way into museums or been traded for profit. The ancestors of the American Indians and other native peoples, such as the Australian Aborigines, have been particular objects of scientific curiosity. The descendants of these peoples object that their human remains still find their way into the curio cabinets of collectors.

To their former owners, many of these objects had been sacred: Egyptian mummies, South American shrunken heads, and skeletons from Australia.

Such objects are still sold in art auctions, despite popular outrage at the practice.

Among American Indians funeral rites are intended to ensure that the souls of the dead remain at peace. Some tribes therefore believe that disturbing graves can harm the living as well as the dead. To ensure that their dead rest in peace,

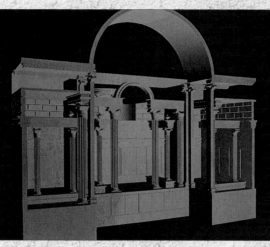

Rediscovering Pompeii
Computers now play a significant role in the study and restoration of archeological sites. This reconstruction of a Pompeian building from the first century was done with the help of a computer.

Indians have begun to demand the return of their remains from museums all over the world, so that they can be reburied with proper religious rites.

Many archeologists agree that 19th-century human remains should be returned to their descendants for burial. Yet they would prefer to continue to study the most ancient bones, which in some cases are over 30,000 years old.

Community property

In Australia, Aboriginal leaders and archeologists have hammered out a compromise to allow remains found at Lake Mungo to be studied. These remains have been radiocarbon-dated to between 30,000 and 24,000 B.C. They were handed back to the local community in 1992 and are stored in a safe, where with the permission of the local people, they can be studied by scientists.

Such compromises may allow modern archeologists to learn more about the past by affording contact with the living descendants of the people they are studying. Most peoples also recognize that archeology can fill in gaps in their history, helping them to understand their ancestors and their past.

THE RESTLESS DEAD

Archeologists have often behaved in a cavalier fashion with the dead. Graves have been plundered and bodies exhumed, dissected, and displayed in museums.

The greatest find in Egyptian archeology was the discovery of the tomb of Tutankhamen in 1922 by the British archeologists Howard Carter and Lord Carnarvon. Some of their methods would no longer be used today because they destroyed valuable historical evidence.

Unfit for a pharaoh

The treatment of the body of the Egyptian pharaoh, Tutankhamen, was particularly grotesque. To remove the mummy from the coffin, the pharaoh's head was removed, the torso cut in half, and the arms and legs amputated. The forearms were severed so that the pharaoh's gold bracelets could be removed. The arms and legs were also cut into sections at the joints to reveal the ends of the long bones in order to find out how old Tutankhamen had been when he died. By any standards, this shows a startling lack of respect for the dead, but it is by no means unique in the chronicles of archeology.

PHOTOGRAPHIC SOURCES